Reason, Truth and God

Reason, Truth and God

Renford Bambrough

METHUEN & CO LTD

6-85

First published in 1969
by Methuen & Co, Ltd
11 New Fetter Lane, London EC4

First published as a University Paperback 1973
© 1969 Renford Bambrough

Printed in Great Britain
by The Camelot Press Ltd,
London and Southampton

SBN 416 70240 6

Distributed in the USA by
HARPER & ROW PUBLISHERS, INC.
BARNES & NOBLE IMPORT DIVISION

Contents

Preface

This book is based on eight Stanton Lectures given at Cambridge during the Lent and Easter Terms of 1963. In preparing the book I have closely followed the order and contents of the outline notes from which the lectures were delivered, and though I have occasionally developed points which were less fully treated in the lectures I have made no attempt to disguise the origins of the book.

The Stanton Lectures of 1964 and 1965 will not be published as such, but the preparation of them has helped me substantially in the writing of a book on ethics and a larger work on metaphysics which will appear in due course. At some places in the present book I have found it convenient to make use of conclusions for which a fuller argument will be offered in these other writings. In the Bibliography I have included a few references to articles in which I have already discussed some of the topics of this book.

I am grateful to many for many things, and I record here my thanks to all who have helped me. My main philosophical debts are acknowledged in the text. I should like to add a special word of thanks to Mr Roy Stone for his help in the process of turning notes into a text; to Mrs Daphne Field for the skill and patience with which she worked from a manuscript so illegible that much of it had to be dictated before it could be typed; and to Professor Donald MacKinnon for his many kindnesses to me during my tenure of the Stanton Lectureship.

RENFORD BAMBROUGH

St John's College,
Cambridge.
August, 1968

TO ERIC IRVINE JOHNSTON

1 · Knowledge

There is a primrose path whose name is Prolegomena – the
shortest way to hell for any audience. I promise to come very
soon to my main business of giving what Wittgenstein, in the
Preface to the *Philosophical Investigations*, calls 'sketches of
landscapes'. I shall be dealing, as concretely and specifically as
possible, with particular examples of theological affirmations
and of philosophical remarks about them. But first I should
like to be allowed to view the whole terrain from a greater
height and a greater distance.

Some of you know already, and soon you will all know, that
I am no theologian. There are some kinds of lectures on the
philosophy of religion that only a theologian is qualified to give.
But it is a mark of the variety and multiplicity of the inquiries
of which 'philosophy of religion' is the family name that there
are other kinds of lectures on the subject that can properly be
given by a philosopher who has no special theological learning.
One important task that falls within this category is that of
explaining the application to religion and its philosophy of
philosophical doctrines and techniques which have been
developed – as most philosophical doctrines and techniques are
nowadays developed – by philosophers who are not primarily,
if at all, concerned with theology and religion.

Every important change in general philosophy is important
for the philosophy of religion, and it is well known, if not
notorious, that in this century there have been some dramatic
changes in general philosophy. My primary purpose in these
lectures is to apply these recent developments to topics in
the philosophy of religion and the philosophy of life. I also
have a secondary purpose, but one which I believe to be not
only important in itself, but also highly relevant to the primary
purpose. By applying recent general philosophy to the philosophy of religion we can come to a better understanding of the
nature and value of recent general philosophy itself. Religious

thinking is such a central and fundamental kind of thinking that any epistemology, any theory about the nature of knowledge and thought and reasoning, which does not provide or suggest some account of the nature of religious thinking and inquiry is under the reasonable suspicion of being at best incomplete, and at worst downright mistaken.

I believe that the work of philosophers in this century has provided us with an account of the nature of reasoning and knowledge which is both comprehensive in its scope and correct in its main conclusions. I will outline this theory, and apply it to the particular and important case of religious knowledge. Many useful accounts of recent philosophy are already available, and some valuable progress has been made in the application of it to the philosophy of religion. It would be generally agreed that there is great scope for further work in this field. It may not be so readily agreed – though I believe it to be true and will argue it in this lecture – that one of the obstacles to further progress in this task has been that contemporary general philosophy itself has not been clearly enough set out or thoroughly enough understood and absorbed even by most professional philosophers, and even by some of the philosophers who are most closely identified, both in their own minds and in those of their readers, with the recent developments of which I am speaking.

Two of the most familiar, insistent and plausible of the many complaints that have been made against Wittgenstein and his pupils and successors are these:

1 That they ignore the large questions about the scope and limits of human knowledge that have exercised the philosophers of the past for two thousand years or more;
2 that they neglect the questions about human life, human virtue and human happiness which many earlier philosophers, including many of the greatest thinkers, regarded as falling firmly within their province, side by side with the technical questions of metaphysics and epistemology.

The first charge is simply false. Wittgenstein and his successors have given answers to just those very questions that have always preoccupied professional, specialized philosophers: Do we know anything? Is it *possible* to know anything? What do we know? How do we know what we know? What is knowledge? What is understanding? What is reasoning? What is proof, truth, justification? Is all knowledge of one kind, or of a small and specifiable number of kinds, or of a large and indefinite number of kinds? Of *what* kind or kinds is knowledge? What are the *objects* of knowledge? In answering these questions Wittgenstein and his successors have set before us a theory of the nature of human thought and knowledge which, whether it is true or false, can certainly bear comparison for scope, generality, interest and importance with any metaphysical or epistemological theory that has been offered in any place at any time. But the authors of this theory have concealed its scope and generality from many of their readers, and sometimes even from themselves, by the idiom in which they have expressed the theory. If it is set out in a different idiom, in an idiom more nearly like that of the traditional metaphysical theories that it claims to supersede, then its scope and its generality, its interest and its importance can be revealed. Wittgenstein's own remark that his activity was 'one of the heirs of the subject that used to be called philosophy', and the insistence of his followers that he inaugurated a 'revolution in philosophy', have combined to encourage both his defenders and his detractors to exaggerate the differences between his work and that of his predecessors. Innovators in philosophy are always tempted to exaggerate the novelty of their work to a point where they are in danger of contradicting their own claims to have answered the very questions that their predecessors had laboured and failed to answer. Philosophy is a continuing conversation, and the latest contributions to it, however striking and original, remain relevant to remarks made earlier and in other languages or tones of voice.

Wittgenstein's work is closely connected with that of his predecessors. Most of the problems he dealt with can be identified as the traditional problems of philosophy, and his doctrines can be set out in ways that reveal them to be answers to those problems. His 'remarks' are not a set of scattered observations; they amount to a comprehensive and coherent system of philosophy.

The second charge is also false, but not so simply or straightforwardly false. It is true that most recent philosophers have neglected questions about human life and human happiness, questions of morality and politics and the philosophy of life, as opposed to questions about the epistemology of morals and politics. What is not true is that the nature of contemporary philosophy itself *requires* that these questions should be neglected by contemporary philosophers, that its techniques are incapable of being applied to such questions.

There is an understandable but regrettable and unnecessary fear on the part of contemporary philosophers of being accused of or credited with any desire to preach or moralize. One of the achievements of recent philosophy has been to make plain the great differences between the technical and specialized questions of epistemology (including the epistemology of morals, politics and religion) and the substantive questions of morals and politics and religion themselves. In their concern to emphasize these important distinctions, and to criticize the misconceived attempts of some earlier thinkers to derive philosophies of life and conduct directly from metaphysical premises by metaphysical arguments, they have overlooked the important connection between metaphysics and these other inquiries – the very connection that led their predecessors to overlook the distinction – and that is that similar techniques of thought are called for by both kinds of inquiry. It is as though mathematicians were so anxious to emphasize the distinction between mathematics and the natural sciences or technology that they refused to countenance the application of their mathematical techniques in the service of physics or engineering.

I shall have more to say about these questions in the last two lectures of this course, under the title of 'Religion and Philosophy of Life'. My present concern is with the first of the two objections that I have mentioned, and I can best approach it by giving an outline account of the theory of knowledge that can be extracted from the writings of Wittgenstein and his successors.

I must be brief, and I must therefore be dogmatic. In this introduction I can offer neither a general defence of Wittgenstein's epistemology nor a systematic explanation of its relevance to theology and religion. In the detail of the later lectures its relevance will be obvious, and the reasons for the theory will emerge more clearly when it is concretely applied to familiar questions and problems.

Every revolution in philosophy has its own conception of the nature of philosophy itself, and of the relations between philosophy and other inquiries and activities. It is here that recent philosophy has achieved its most important results, and here that it is most liable to misunderstanding and misrepresentation. It is here, too, that it stands in greatest need of clarification, and, I believe, of some measure of modification and correction. For our present purpose there are special advantages in beginning with questions about the nature of philosophy. The application to theology and religion of any philosophical system is very closely bound up with the view that the system offers of the nature of philosophy itself and of its external relations with other inquiries. The special difficulties and problems of the philosophy of philosophy are calculated to reveal the virtues and the defects of any system of philosophy that is applied to them. Finally (and although this is less important now it will be of great importance in the lectures on religion and philosophy of life) it is the most characteristic features of their doctrines about the relations between philosophical and non-philosophical inquiries that have led many present-day philosophers to neglect substantive questions about human life and human happiness, about vice and virtue, about political and social problems.

The main questions *about* philosophy are among the oldest questions *of* philosophy. Is philosophy the queen of the sciences, or their humble handmaid? Is it the foundation of the structure of our knowledge, or the coping-stone? Does philosophy have a subject-matter of its own, or a method of its own, or neither, or both? Is it the business of philosophers to provide an overall world-picture, to collect and codify the results of other disciplines, or is it rather to deal with questions that arise at the very beginning of every search for knowledge, in such a sense that philosophical conclusions, or at least philosophical assumptions or presuppositions, are necessary as starting-points before we can embark on the study of any non-philosophical question?

In trying to answer these questions I shall be giving an account in my own terms, and with few quotations or references, of a system of philosophy which is largely not my own. It is one which owes a great debt to Wittgenstein and his successors, and especially to the work of Professor Wisdom.

Metaphysics, or pure philosophy, is the study of the nature of knowledge, the nature of reasons, and the nature of truth, verification and justification. Its task is to compare and contrast the various kinds of knowledge, and the various kinds of reasons and justifications that can be given for them. Since this is an inquiry into the nature of grounds, and reasons, and propositions, it is an *a priori*, logical inquiry; but it is not a *deductive* inquiry, like formal logic and mathematics. In metaphysics or pure philosophy we are concerned with *ultimate* justification, and therefore not with the ways in which propositions of a given type support propositions of that same type, but with the ways in which propositions of one type are supported by propositions of other types. No proposition has as its ultimate ground a proposition or set of propositions of the same logical type as itself.

The clearest evidence that ultimate justification always involves a transition from propositions of one type to propositions of another type is provided by the arguments of philosophical sceptics. The sceptic about our knowledge of the external world makes plain that propositions about the external world ultimately depend, not on other propositions about the external world, but on propositions about human experience. He rightly rejects any attempt to justify one proposition about the external world by basing it on other propositions about the external world: his scepticism is a scepticism about the whole category or kind of propositions about material things, and to offer him some propositions of that kind in support of other propositions of that kind would be to beg the question against him.

The traditional problem of induction exhibits the same pattern. Propositions about the future depend in the end on propositions which are not about the future, but about the present and the past. The sceptic about induction points out that propositions about the future do not logically follow from propositions about the present and the past. But if, when he challenges a particular conclusion about the future, we support it by premises which are also about the future, and from which the conclusion does logically follow, he will rightly ask how we know that our *premises* are true.

The same pattern recurs in all the familiar and traditional disputes of metaphysics. Propositions about the minds of others ultimately depend on propositions about bodily behaviour, from which they do not logically follow. No moral proposition logically follows from any set of premises that does not include at least one moral proposition. It follows that if we base a moral proposition on a set of premises from which it logically follows we are begging the question against the sceptic about morality. Causal propositions do not logically follow from the propositions about conjunctions between events that are the ultimate grounds for causal propositions. Whenever we try to meet the challenge of a sceptic we seem to be doomed to offer him either something that is not strong enough to support the conclusion that he questions, or something so strong that it is itself of the same kind as the proposition that he questions, and will therefore be questioned on the same grounds.

Metaphysics, or pure philosophy, or epistemology – I shall use these terms interchangeably – is the study of the logical relations between propositions and their ultimate grounds, in the sense of 'ultimate grounds' that is indicated by these examples of sceptical arguments.

When this study is undertaken for its own sake, as it is by most contemporary philosophers, it is a *pure* study in the sense in which mathematics is a pure study when it is undertaken for its own sake, and not with a view to any application outside its own sphere. But just as mathematics may be applied, so also is it possible, and sometimes useful, to apply the principles of pure philosophy in the search for answers to questions which are not themselves philosophical. The engineer, the physicist, and the applied mathematician make use of the techniques and the results of the pure mathematician: but when they do so they are not primarily engaged in *mathematical* inquiry. Their primary purpose is not to develop further the pure *a priori* principles that are elicited and enunciated by the pure mathematician, but to apply them to non-mathematical phenomena with a view to throwing light on those phenomena themselves.

The techniques and the results of the pure philosopher are also capable of being applied to the treatment of non-philosophical questions. The pure *a priori* principles that are elicited and enunciated by the pure philosopher are the principles which are used by thinkers about non-philosophical questions: by scientists and historians and moralists and theologians and critics.

The most striking cases of the application of the methods and principles of pure philosophy to the treatment of non-philosophical questions are found in the work of radical innovators who are reassessing and calling in question the most fundamental concepts of their own disciplines. Freud was concerned with questions about the nature of the human mind. His study was an empirical study, a study of the actual, of man as he is. But in the course of pursuing this study he found it useful to reflect on the *a priori*, philosophical question, 'What is a wish?' or 'What is an unconscious state of mind?' or 'Is it conceivable that there should be such a thing as an unconscious state of mind?' When he reflected on these and similar questions he was reflecting philosophically: he was not only using the techniques of the philosopher, but using them on questions that belong to pure philosophy. But he was doing philosophy with a view to making progress in psychology, as the engineer and the physicist do mathematics with a view to solving problems or making discoveries in engineering or physics.

Einstein's primary concern was with physics, with questions about the natural world, and not with philosophy. But in the course of investigating nature he found it useful to reflect on the *a priori*, philosophical question, 'What is it to verify that a certain event takes place at a certain place at a certain time?' and on the *a priori*, philosophical question, 'What is simultaneity? What is it to establish that two events take place at the *same* time?' Einstein has rightly been called a 'philosopher-scientist', and one might speak of Freud as a 'philosopher-psychologist'. They both engaged in philosophy, but they used their philosophy to serve the purposes of their science. They were applied philosophers, not pure philosophers.

Even the pure mathematician may have occasion to engage in applied philosophy. Progress in the study of transfinite numbers was helped by reflection on the philosophical questions, 'What is a number?' and 'Are infinite numbers numbers?'

When we speak of a 'mathematical physicist' we have in mind a man whose questions and results belong to physics, but whose training, talent and technique are mathematical.

This way of speaking suggests a way of describing the distinction between pure and applied philosophy. We may contrast *philosophical* science, *philosophical* theology, *philosophical* morality, with philosophy *of* science, philosophy *of* theology, philosophy *of* morality. The first of each of these pairs is a branch of applied philosophy; the second of each pair is a branch of pure philosophy or metaphysics. The applied philosopher uses philosophical techniques in the course of an inquiry whose questions are non-philosophical. The pure philosopher studies the nature of the questions and answers, methods and arguments, concepts and propositions, that are used by himself and by other specialized inquirers, and by himself and others in their everyday, non-specialized reflections and deliberations.

In recognizing the important connection between pure and applied philosophy that is marked by calling them both 'philosophy' we must beware of obscuring an equally important distinction between them: that each of them is logically independent of the other, in the sense that no result arrived at by either of them can count in favour of, or against, or can entail, or can contradict, any result that may be arrived at by the other.

The idea of logical independence is well illustrated by the parallel case of the distinction between pure and applied mathematics. No proposition of pure mathematics depends for its truth on any proposition about the physical world, and *vice versa*. The function of mathematical principles in the inquiry of the physicist is to serve as routes by which he travels from physical propositions to other physical propositions. Mathematical propositions serve the natural scientist as principles of inference and not as premises.

The propositions of pure philosophy are similarly related to the substantive propositions of the various inquiries in and to which philosophy may be applied. The pure philosopher may explain what it is to verify a proposition of physics or psychology, but to know *how to verify* a proposition is quite different from knowing *that it is* verified or falsified. The pure philosopher's knowledge, like that of the pure mathematician, is knowledge of the logical relations between propositions. It is always expressible in hypothetical form: and there is all the difference in the world between knowing what *would* be the case *if* something else were the case, and knowing what is *as a*

matter of fact the case. I may know that if all antelopes have
cloven hoofs and Bucephalus is an antelope then Bucephalus has
cloven hoofs without knowing whether all antelopes have cloven
hoofs or whether Bucephalus is an antelope. And many a problem
from a school text-book of mathematics or from the puzzle-
page of a magazine will show that I may have all the premises
I need for drawing a certain conclusion without knowing
whether that conclusion is warranted by those premises.

Pure philosophy is neutral on all questions that do not belong
to pure philosophy: it has nothing to tell us about the world or
life or man or God. The propositions of pure philosophy refer to the
logical characters of propositions, and to characterize a proposition is also to characterize the contradictory of that proposition,
to explain how it could be settled whether it is the proposition or
its contradictory that is true. But to *use* the procedures described
by the pure philosopher requires not only the principles of
inference that he describes but also *premises* which are not
provided by philosophical reflection.

When we understand that pure and applied philosophy are
mutually independent, and why they are mutually independent, we may be in danger of falling into another misunderstanding. The two inquiries are mutually independent, but they are
not mutually irrelevant.

Here there is scope for the application of what I have called
'Ramsey's Maxim', that wherever there is a violent and per-
sistent philosophical dispute there is likely to be a false assumption that is shared by the conflicting parties (F. P. Ramsey,
The Foundations of Mathematics, pp. 115–16). The critics and the
defenders of contemporary philosophy are liable to join together in the mistaken assumption that pure philosophy can
have no relevance to the substantive questions and propositions
of science and history and morality and politics and religion if
it is logically independent of them. The critics insist on the
relevance of pure philosophy to the important questions asked
by men who are not philosophers, and take it as showing that
philosophy and other inquiries are *not* mutually independent.
Those who defend the thesis that philosophy is neutral on non-
philosophical issues feel bound to conclude that philosophy is
wholly irrelevant to such issues. But mutual relevance is not
incompatible with logical independence, as may be seen by

looking again at the parallel case of pure and applied mathematics. Mathematical inquiry is clearly not irrelevant to physical inquiry, although no physical proposition can be established by purely mathematical reasoning and no mathematical proposition can be established by physical investigation.

So far I have spoken only of the aims of the pure philosopher, and not of his methods. How is his task to be carried out? How are we to pursue the philosopher's purpose of characterizing the kinds of knowledge and their ultimate grounds, and the relations of one kind of knowledge with another? Wittgenstein's own answer is that the method of philosophy is *descriptive*; that philosophy proceeds by seeking and providing detailed descriptions of concrete particular instances of knowledge and its grounds. Professor Wisdom has supplemented Wittgenstein's answer by showing how valuable for the philosopher's purpose are some techniques which are not straightforwardly descriptive, but which characterize the modes of knowledge by means of paradox, portraiture or even caricature.

Here it becomes important to see the application to the conduct of metaphysical philosophy of Wittgenstein's own treatment of one of the principal problems of traditional philosophy – the problem of universals. Wittgenstein recommended and used a technique of detailed, concrete description, as an alternative to the dangerous method that philosophers had for so long followed, of trying to reduce to formulae, to statements of strict criteria, of necessary and sufficient conditions, the accounts that they wished to offer of the nature of knowledge in general, or of this or that particular kind of knowledge. He complained that philosophers had shown 'a contemptuous attitude towards the particular case', that under the obsessive influence of a 'craving for generality' they had both misdescribed and misconducted the business of philosophy.

From the time of Socrates onwards philosophers have been in the habit of seeking definitions, of insisting that 'one must define one's terms'. The plausible assumptions that feed this obsessive desire for definitions and formulae can be displayed and clarified by considering the structure of Plato's Socratic dialogues.

Socrates begins by asking 'What is piety?' or 'What is bravery?' or 'What is knowledge?' Euthyphro or Laches or

Theaetetus offers examples: 'Piety is what I am doing now, in prosecuting even my own father for murder'; 'Bravery is standing fast and not running away'; 'Knowledge is shoe-making, and geometry, and so on'. Socrates is dissatisfied: he explains that he is looking for a general account of the nature of piety or bravery or knowledge, and not a mere list of examples. He is asking for a statement of what is common and peculiar to all the instances that fall under the general term in question. What is the common nature or common form or character of all the instances, by which they are distinguished from everything to which the term does *not* apply? He needs to know the meaning of 'knowledge' or 'justice' in the sense in which we know the meaning of the word 'surface' when we know that every surface is the limit of a solid and that every limit of a solid is a surface. His friends must try again.

Socrates is now presented with suggestions that conform to his requirements, with proposed *definitions*: 'Justice consists in giving every man his due'; 'Knowledge is correct belief'; 'Piety is doing what is pleasing to the gods'. These answers are in the *form* that Socrates requires: they are attempts to say what is in common to all the instances of justice and knowledge and piety. Unfortunately, however, they are *mistaken* definitions. Socrates is able to produce a decisive counter-example to each of them, and to every new definition that is suggested. He is always able to point *either* to something that undoubtedly *is* an instance of the relevant kind, but which does not satisfy the proposed criterion, *or* to something that satisfies the proposed criterion, but which is undoubtedly *not* of the relevant kind. Sometimes the brave man runs away. Sometimes it would be unjust to restore a man's own sword to him, even if we had solemnly promised to do so.

'What curious people we are,' says Socrates. 'We use words like "friendship" and "justice" and "virtue" every day and with every confidence: and yet it turns out, when we carefully consider the matter, that we do not know what these words mean.' Each of the early Socratic dialogues, and the *Theaetetus*, which is constructed on the same pattern, accordingly ends in ἀπορία – in deadlock and perplexity, in 'not knowing where to turn'.

The Socratic search for definitions depends on two assumptions which Socrates repeatedly and explicitly invokes, and which have been implicit in the practice of most philosophers at most times: (1) that there is no justification for applying a general term to its instances unless the instances have something in common other than that they are its instances, and (2) that nobody knows the meaning of a general term unless he is able to *say* what it means, i.e. to state what it is that the instances have in common and in virtue of which they are its instances.

Wittgenstein rightly rejected these two assumptions. His remarks about 'family resemblances', and about 'games', 'language', 'knowledge', and innumerable other examples, enable us to see that the resemblances between the instances that fall under a general term may 'overlap and criss-cross' in such a way as to defeat any attempt to offer a formula which will *both* express what is common and peculiar to the instances *and* explain the meaning of the general term.

There is controversy about the range and scope of the point made by Wittgenstein's family resemblances analogy; about whether it was meant to apply to *all* general terms, or only to a limited number of special terms, such as 'game' and 'number' and 'language'. For my present purpose it is sufficient to notice that the concept of knowledge is treated by Wittgenstein himself as a 'family resemblances' concept, and to sum up his doctrine by reference to that concept in particular.

The *Theaetetus* itself provides all the material that we need. For although Socrates fails to do what he is explicitly trying to do, he nevertheless makes a notable contribution to our understanding of the nature of knowledge, and he does so by using just the method that Wittgenstein recommends: by considering *examples*. Every proposed definition of knowledge that has any plausibility is based on a review of some of the most typical cases of knowledge, and the refutation of a proposed definition consists in pointing to examples of knowledge that are not covered by the definition, or to examples that are covered by the definition but are not cases of knowledge. By this dialectical method Socrates and his friends provide themselves with a surer and deeper grasp of the scope and limits of the concept of knowledge.

At the end of the dialogue Socrates speaks of failure and ἀπορία only because he has misconceived and misdescribed the nature of the inquiry in which he was engaged; and his misconception is a direct consequence of the two assumptions that Wittgenstein rejects. For (1) it is the extreme variety and multiplicity of the cases of knowledge, the lack of a single element common to all of them, the fact that the concept has such a complex internal structure, that defeats all attempts to sum it up in a sentence, and (2) it is the fact that Socrates and Theaetetus can already distinguish cases to which the term 'knowledge' applies from cases to which it does not apply that makes it possible for them to propound plausible definitions and to refute them.

Socrates mistakenly identifies the question 'What is knowledge?' with the question 'What is the *definition* of knowledge?', and hence supposes that his failure to produce a definition is a failure to say what knowledge is. But the procedure by which he arrives at this conclusion shows both that there is no true and non-trivial definition of knowledge and that Socrates and Theaetetus already know what knowledge is without knowing of any brief formula that sums up their knowledge of what knowledge is.

Even if there were a correct and useful definition of knowledge, it would not be a means, and still less a necessary means, to knowing what knowledge is, since one would need to have a complete grasp of all the cases of knowledge, and of their relations to each other and to everything that is not knowledge, *before* one could know that the definition was correct.

To establish that knowledge is not identical with perception, or with correct opinion, or with correct opinion plus a λόγος, or with anything but knowledge, is both to reveal and to deepen and extend a deep and extensive understanding of what knowledge is. It is also to show that there is *nothing* that is common and peculiar to all cases of knowledge except that they are all cases of knowledge, and that one can know what knowledge is without *already* being able to *say* what knowledge is. Knowing what knowledge is is a necessary precondition of being able to say what it is, and not *vice versa*: a definition of knowledge is not only impossible, it is also unnecessary.

These conclusions may be neatly underlined by noticing that the practice of Socrates himself is different from and better than his theory. When Laches, Lysis, Charmides, Meno and

Theaetetus try to explain the meaning of general terms by presenting examples, Socrates, with vociferous support from Platonic commentators, tells them that they are facing in the wrong direction. As Wittgenstein says (*The Blue Book*, p. 20), 'When Socrates asks the question, "what is knowledge?" he does not even regard it as a *preliminary* answer to enumerate cases of knowledge.' But when Socrates asks for a definition instead of mere examples, and Theaetetus asks for an explanation of what a *definition* is, Socrates does not *define* definition: *he gives examples*. And now the commentators are silent.

The problem of universals is a problem about classification, about what it is for a number of *different* things to be of the *same* kind. In ancient times it was called 'the problem of the one and the many': the problem of justifying the application to *many* different instances of *one* general name. The philosopher's task is to classify instances of knowledge, to describe and portray the nature of the various *kinds* of knowledge and reasoning, as well as to show in what sense, if any, the many varieties of knowledge amount to one single, unified kind. To accept Wittgenstein's account of the nature of universals and generality, instead of the traditional Socratic assumptions, is therefore to arrive at a different view from that of most earlier philosophers of the nature of the tasks and tools of philosophy. Wittgenstein's suggestion that the method of philosophy is detailed description of concrete cases is cut from the same cloth as his theory of universals.

The history of metaphysics and epistemology confirms Wittgenstein's diagnosis. The dangers of looking for general definitions, and the value of testing philosophical theories by applying them to concrete particular cases, are equally striking whether we are concerned with knowledge in general or with some particular kind of knowledge. Whether we are asking 'What is knowledge?' or 'What is scientific knowledge?', 'What is theological knowledge?', 'What is moral knowledge?', it will in either case be impossible to find a correct answer of the form that Socrates required. A philosopher who does not recognize that such a search is misguided is subject to two very different but equally serious dangers. He may, like Socrates, recognize his failure to answer the question 'What is the definition of knowledge?' and either despair of making any progress in answering the question 'What is knowledge?' or redouble his misguided efforts; or he may believe that he has succeeded in his search, and may thus accept as an accurate account of the nature of knowledge one that distorts and misrepresents its nature.

Among the mistaken theories whose plausibility is mainly derived from the mistaken assumptions of Socrates there are two types of doctrine that deserve particular notice here, partly because they are the most frequent, and the most far reaching in their philosophical ill-effects, and partly because they are specially liable to involve misrepresentation of theological reasoning and knowledge. These two types of theory are Scepticism and Positivism.

Scepticism flows naturally from the assumption that there is a formula or definition in which the common essence of all cases and types of knowledge can be summed up. A philosopher who makes this assumption, but who is otherwise an acute and unprejudiced observer of the traits and characters of the various kinds of knowledge, will notice how radically one kind of knowledge differs from another: physics from mathematics, mathematics from psychology, psychology from morality. He will see that no neat and simple account of the nature of knowledge will embrace all these inquiries. Since he is attached to his neat and simple account, he will consistently conclude that some of these branches of knowledge are *not* branches of *knowledge* at all. Instead of enlarging his conception of knowledge he will refuse to accept as an example of knowledge anything that does not conform to his narrow conception.

Even if the sceptic does not explicitly commit himself to a restrictive definition of knowledge, his arguments against the claim of some particular branch of knowledge to be a branch of knowledge will usually presuppose that nothing can be a branch of knowledge unless it conforms to a narrow specification. The most characteristic form of sceptical argument is one which condemns one branch of knowledge because it lacks the characteristic features of some other branch of knowledge which the sceptic has implicitly or explicitly adopted as a *paradigm* of knowledge. Sceptics about our knowledge of the external world contrast it unfavourably with our knowledge of our own minds or with mathematical and logical knowledge. Scepticism about induction is usually based on a contrast between knowledge of the future and knowledge of the present and the past. The same points of logical contrast between propositions about the past, the present and the future have sometimes been used in support of scepticism about the past. Morality and theology have been held to be too unlike physics and mathematics to be included with them under the concepts of knowledge and rational inquiry. These and most other sceptical theories have been based on accurate observations of the points of difference between one branch of knowledge and another, together with the mistaken idea that such differences are too great to allow the contrasted branches to fall under the same concept.

The only scepticism which can defend itself without the use of points of contrast between one branch of knowledge and another is *absolute* scepticism, the thesis that there is *no* knowledge of *any* kind. But this view is itself based on the same assumptions as the more limited forms of scepticism which reject one kind of knowledge by contrasting it with another. For the absolute sceptic either expressly insists on or silently presupposes a single pattern to which what is claimed to be a branch of knowledge must conform. When he sees that no branch of knowledge matches his blueprint, he rejects all branches of knowledge instead of abandoning his blueprint. Absolute scepticism can be defended only by the most extreme of all departures from the descriptive method recommended by Wittgenstein. Instead of describing the nature of knowledge by presenting particular instances in all their variety, the absolute sceptic assumes in advance that there is a single, simple pattern in all the instances, and when he applies his preconceived pattern to the instances, he is impelled to reject the instances because they do not fit the pattern, whereas the variety of the instances is just what shows that his pattern is mistaken.

Positivist theories may be discussed even more briefly, for they are no more than special cases of some of the limited sceptical theories, and they depend on the same prior assumptions. The positivist, like the sceptic, notices the differences between mathematics and the natural sciences, his chosen paradigms of knowledge, and morality, theology and metaphysics; he then, like the sceptic, rejects the recalcitrant instances which do not conform to his preconceived picture of the essence of knowledge. He does not even apply consistently the sceptical method by which he arrives at his results; for the differences between mathematics and the natural sciences are, as the sceptic of the senses makes clear, as radical as the differences between either of them and any of the branches of knowledge that the positivist rejects. Scepticism of the senses is positivism without its inhibitions.

The assumptions that lead to sceptical or positivist mis-representations of the character of knowledge as a whole have also and repeatedly led philosophers to misconceive and mis-describe the nature of particular branches of knowledge. The criss-crossing patterns of connections and distinctions between one kind of knowledge and another not only defeat attempts to give a neat and compendious account of the whole nature of knowledge; they also make it impossible to give a brief and tidy definition of any particular kind of knowledge. Knowledge in general is to be characterized by describing instances of know-ledge; a particular kind of knowledge is to be characterized by describing instances of that kind; and in both cases it is import-ant that the instances should be many and varied, that they should not be selected to conform to a preconceived blueprint.

Moral philosophy and the philosophy of science provide salutary examples of the dangers of a craving for unity and simplicity. Many mistaken accounts of the nature of moral reasoning have resulted from a search for the *essence* of morality, for a feature or conjunction of features common and peculiar to all cases of moral knowledge, moral argument and moral judgement. A philosopher who is in pursuit of the 'essentially moral' element in morality sees his task as like that of removing impurities from an ore in order to isolate a pure specimen of a mineral. A good example is provided by Hume's celebrated remark that 'After every circumstance, every relation is known, the understanding has no further room to operate, nor any object on which it could employ itself' (*Enquiries*, § 240). Hume sees that factual inquiry and logical inquiry are distinct from moral inquiry, and concludes that they cannot therefore constitute part of the nature of moral inquiry; that the moral character of a moral dispute resides wholly in what remains when all factual and logical disputes have been settled, and no scope remains for reason, but only for the passions and the sentiments. Hume has been followed in this as in some other respects by positivist and emotivist theorists of ethics. But this mistake is not confined to Hume and his empiricist successors. The intuitionist in ethics – Prichard or Bradley – presents a moral theory whose structure is closely similar to that of the empiricist theory, because he, too, wishes to isolate the specifically moral element in morality, and to exclude from the scope of morality all that belongs to non-moral inquiries. It is as though one were to argue that flour and sugar have nothing to do with what makes a chocolate cake a chocolate cake, because these ingredients also occur in ginger cakes and vanilla cakes. Not even a chocolate cake can be made of nothing but chocolate; and chocolate is in any case found in biscuits and puddings as well as in cakes.

The question 'What is science?' has all too often been treated as if it were the question 'What is the definition of science?', and then answered in such a way as to deny the title of science to many of the sciences. Sometimes a particular science, such as physics, is adopted as a paradigm to which all other sciences must conform. This line of approach leads to the dismissal of much of botany and zoology as 'mere natural history – not really *science*'. Sometimes a particular element in the nature of one or more sciences is cast as the essentially scientific element in all sciences. Those who present *prediction* as being the essence of science are led either to deny that geology and palaeontology are sciences or to misrepresent them as essentially predictive. And such an account does not even do justice to physics, which is its own chosen paradigm. However important the predictive element in physics may be, there have been theoretical achievements in physics whose value was disproportionate to the importance of the new predictions that they warranted. A man might have Galileo's power of predicting the behaviour of balls rolling down inclined planes without having Galileo's grasp of the relationship between the acceleration and the angle of inclination.

These are no more than a small selection of the cases in which metaphysicians and epistemologists have been misled by *essentialist* assumptions, and I have given no more than a crude sketch of each example. But it is already clear that in our inquiry into the nature of theology we must be suspicious on principle of any neat account which maintains that theology *is* or *is essentially* this or that or the other thing. We shall do well to remember the excellent reasons given by William James, in Lecture II of *The Varieties of Religious Experience*, for refusing to offer a definition of 'religion'. James was well aware, as too many enquirers in the philosophy of religion and in other branches of philosophy have failed to be aware, that an accurate account of something intricate and complex cannot be presented in neat and tidy terms; that the imposition of a single, simple framework on religion or government or science can lead only to distortion and misrepresentation, and to conflicts between rival distortions, with each theorist claiming to see the whole essence of a complex nature in one element that he has isolated and emphasized.

But it will also be useful to us to remember how much Socrates contributed to the answering of the question 'What is knowledge?' when he expressed it in the misleading form 'What is the definition of knowledge?' A philosopher who is trying to define the indefinable helps us to understand the nature of what he is trying to define: for his definition would not be plausible enough to tempt him if it did not pick out, as the supposed 'essence' of knowledge or religion or morality, something that is importantly *characteristic* of knowledge or religion or morals. And to look at the rival definitions, to trace the lines of conflict between them, to set one partial view beside another, may help us to achieve a more complete understanding. This lesson is underlined and elaborated by Professor Wisdom in his paper 'A Feature of Wittgenstein's Technique' (*Paradox and Discovery*, pp. 90–103). He quotes and endorses William James's warning, but he also warns us that a distaste for oversimplification can itself be too *simpliste*. Definitions may not be either necessary or sufficient for philosophical purposes; correct definitions may be possible only at a stage at which they are also unnecessary; but it does not follow that the Socratic search for definitions is not *one* of the ways that lead to *some* of the understanding that we seek.

James is far from being the only or the earliest philosopher before Wittgenstein to diagnose the dangers of the craving for unity, simplicity and generality. Aristotle preached and practised the importance of recognizing that one inquiry differs in nature and procedure from another. He looked at each branch of knowledge, as he looked at each species of plant and animal, to trace its own distinctive lineaments without hindrance by the imposition of any predetermined pattern; and he knew that the character of a species can be known only by attending to the character of its specimens. We must start with τὰ ἐφ’ ἡμῖν – with what is directly available to us and is therefore most clearly seen by us – the particular and the concrete.

Aristotle's insistent polemic against Plato's Theory of Forms points the same moral. From the bold generalization of the theorist an appeal always lies to τὰ καθ’ ἕκαστα, to the cases that are, in Wisdom's phrase, 'the final food of thought'. The doctor's concern is not with 'health-in-itself', but with *this* patient. The moralist, too, deals in details, and the Form of the Good is too abstract and remote to help him.

Aristotle's recognition that there may be great variety among the instances that belong to the same kind is most clearly shown in his doctrine of analogy, whose application to the concept of knowledge adumbrates much of what I have expressed in terms of Wittgenstein's notion of family resemblances. The sceptic and the positivist, Hume and the philosophers of science, have failed to see the epistemological importance of Aristotle's doctrine that not every term which fails to be *univocal* is merely *equivocal*; that between the univocal and the equivocal there lies the *analogical*. The word 'knowledge' is not used in exactly the same way when we speak of moral knowledge, mathematical knowledge and physical knowledge; but it is not being used in three totally unrelated ways. The instances of knowledge are analogically related. It is a mistake to suppose that where there is *one meaning* there must be *one thing* (*Posterior Analytics*, I, 24).

Wittgenstein is said to have thought of using as an epigraph for the *Philosophical Investigations* a sentence from *King Lear*: 'I will teach you differences.' His polemic was constantly directed against the philosopher's habit of feeding on 'a one-sided diet of examples'. He saw philosophy as a process of 'assembling reminders for a particular purpose', and more often than not the reminders were of cases that we had failed to take into account, of *differences* between the present case and other cases which had equal claims to fall under the term or concept of which too simple an account had been offered.

That there is great scope for the application of these principles to problems in the philosophy of religion immediately becomes clear if we consider what logical variety may be found within the compass of a single creed. The statement that Jesus suffered under Pontius Pilate, a statement of historical fact for which the authority of the *Annals* of Tacitus may be quoted, is clearly of a very different logical order from the claim that 'He ascended into Heaven, and sitteth upon the right hand of God'. And even the historical statement may arouse more than purely historical controversy if it is expressed in the form that *Christ* suffered under Pontius Pilate.

Professor Dorothy Emmet, in her British Academy Lecture, 'Presuppositions and Finite Truths' (1949), has made similar points about the subtlety and intricacy of some historical disputes that may seem at first sight much more straightforward than the issues raised by the Apostles' Creed. We might compare and contrast the minimal statement that the head of Charles Stuart was severed from the body of Charles Stuart, with a number of other statements about his death: that *Charles the First* was beheaded; that Charles the First was *judicially executed*; that Charles the First was *murdered*; that Charles the First was *martyred*. All these descriptions purport to be descriptions of the same historical event, but the different formulations carry quite different commitments about the historical, legal and religious questions that cluster round the death of Charles.

In the philosophy of religion, too, we must be constantly aware of the variety of activities, modes of expression and kinds of affirmation that fall under the general headings of religious observance, practice, feeling, experience and thought. Praying and praising, repenting, confessing, absolving, meditating, preaching, exhorting, exegesis, faith and doubt, apologetic, liturgy, sacrament, conversion and lapse: all these fall within the province of a philosopher who sets out to give a comprehensive account of the nature of religion and theology. And here again we must emphasize not only this internal variety, not only the fact that all these very different elements, and many others different again from all or most of them, fall under the same heading of religion, but also the fact that each of them is closely linked with many of the others, as well as with much that falls outside the scope of religion.

We shall not be able to recognize and describe this multiplicity and this complexity, to do justice to these overlappings and criss-crossings, if we are attached to any ready-made scheme according to which this or that element in religion is central and essential, and the others peripheral or extraneous. To think of any one element as *the* essential element, or to dismiss any element as not belonging to the essence of religion because it is not *the* essence, the *whole* essence, of religion, is to take a road that leads to falsehood or to Socratic ἀπορία.

But those who have travelled that dangerous road tell travellers' tales that deserve a hearing. Morality is not the whole of religion; there is more in religion than a belief in the supernatural, or a particular way of looking at nature or at human nature: but some of those who have seen one such element as the whole of religion had good eyesight, and no single element would have hidden from them the importance of the other elements if it did not loom so large on the religious scene that it must still be prominent when looked at in a juster perspective.

But it is high time to leave the primrose path. The metaphysical thesis that metaphysics is best conducted by the examination of concrete and particular cases must itself be defended by the examination of concrete and particular cases. Theology and religion cannot be characterized by dangerously general remarks about the dangers of generality. *Ad scrutinium.*

2 · Olympus

Chairs and tables have been the familiar furniture of the philosophical world for many centuries. The very word 'matter' is a transliteration of the Latin *materia* or *materies*, which is in turn a translation of the Greek ὕλη – wood or timber, that is to say the material out of which furniture is made. The chair in the corner and the tree in the quad have become a bit of a bore after all this time, but we go on with them because they have one almost indispensable qualification for use as examples in the discussion of philosophical problems about perception and our knowledge of the external world, and that is that nobody who was not a philosopher, and no philosopher who was not engaged in doing philosophy, would ever say or think that they did not exist, or that we did not know for certain whether they existed or not. When we are dealing with epistemological questions about *how* we know that they exist, or with onto-logical questions about whether they *really* exist, or with sceptical questions about whether we *really know* that they exist, it is convenient not to have to engage at the same time in non-philosophical controversy about the substantive truth or false-hood of the propositions whose nature and mode of justification we are examining.

It is much the same in moral philosophy. Ross's grave concern with borrowed books that *obviously* ought to be re-turned, and with parcels that obviously ought to be posted, may lay him open to ridicule from those who do not recognize what he is up to, and even to the risk of boring or irritating many who do know what he is up to, but he was right to concentrate on cases of moral judgements which are *morally* unquestionable when he was trying to find out and to explain *what it is* to know that something is right or wrong, good or bad.

It is the same story again when we talk about the philosophy of mathematics or the philosophy of logic. We constantly re-mind ourselves of the mortality of Socrates and of the irrationality of π; we seldom venture further into arithmetic than a five-year-old child could go. We stick to 'two and two make four', for the sound reason that it is difficult enough to explain *how* we know a mathematical proposition to be true, without having to wonder at the same time *whether* we know it to be true.

But when we come to the philosophy of religion, it is not the same story again. We suddenly become very bold, and try to handle at once the most difficult and controversial cases of theological doctrines: the existence of God, the Incarnation, the Resurrection, the doctrine of the Trinity. In all the other branches of philosophy that I have mentioned, and in most of those that I have not mentioned, we choose simple examples so that when we are considering the mode of verification or justi-fication of a class of propositions we shall not have to be both-ered with controversy about the truth or falsehood of some particular member of the class of propositions in question. Why do we not follow the same policy in the philosophy of religion? Why do we not at least *start* with theological proposi-tions that we *know* to be true, just as in the other cases we begin with the chair that we know to be there, the promise that we know we ought to keep, the argument that is unquestionably valid?

The answer seems clear enough: it is just that there *are* no theological propositions that we *know* to be true, or *know* to be false. We feel that we know *nothing* in this field, that it consists entirely of radically controversial questions. And yet this obvious and natural answer is quite wrong. In the philosophy of religion, just as in the philosophy of perception or of morality or of logic and mathematics, there are available to us, if only we are willing to use them, large classes of wholly uncontroversial cases. There are large classes of cases of propositions which are definitely theological and which are also either definitely known to be true or definitely known to be false. I suggest that we should therefore adopt in the case of theological knowledge exactly the policy that we regularly adopt when considering other kinds of knowledge: the policy of taking, as guides to the nature of the kind of knowledge in question, examples of questions to which we should ordinarily and rightly say that we know the answers.

A thorough and systematic pursuit of this policy would

C

involve us in considering, more seriously than I believe any philosopher has ever considered it in this connection, the logical character of a belief in fairies, or witches, or ghosts, or Father Christmas. These beliefs are of course not theological beliefs, but they do share with theological beliefs many of their most important features. I will not pursue these cases any further here, although I believe that the further pursuit of them would be very valuable and instructive from the point of view of the philosophy of religion, because they may seem not to be theological enough, to be too far away from the central cases of Judaic and Christian theology.

But the same objection cannot be made against the cases that I do wish to consider further: namely, questions about the existence and attributes of the ancient Greek gods and goddesses – Zeus, Poseidon and Apollo, Artemis, Athena and Aphrodite. These are quite certainly *divinities*, and discussion of their existence and their nature and activities is certainly therefore theological discussion. And this large and rich class of examples also satisfies the other requirement that I have laid down for myself: we would all ordinarily and unhesitatingly say that we *know* that these gods and goddesses do *not* exist. How do we know that they do not exist? When we are really clear about this question, we shall be better equipped to deal with the more important and more difficult questions that usually occupy the centre of the stage in discussions about the philosophy of religion.

Before I consider some detailed examples of ancient theological beliefs, I will first say something about an objection that might possibly be raised against the approach that I am adopting and recommending in this lecture. It may be said that the theological beliefs of the ancient Greeks are too radically different from the doctrines of the 'higher religions' for a consideration of the former to have any chance of throwing light upon the latter. Isaiah the prophet and the Fourth Evangelist and St Paul, St Anselm and St Augustine and St Thomas Aquinas, Pascal and Kierkegaard and Karl Barth – all these, it may be said, represent such greater profundity and such greater sophistication of religious thought and religious experience than anything to be found among the polytheistic myths of the Greeks and Romans, that to give serious attention to the epistemology of such ancient and such primitive religious beliefs can at best be to tinker ineffectively on the fringes of what really matters to us.

This is already a cogent objection, and it requires an answer before I can proceed. But the objection can be put in a stronger form still. It may be suggested that to talk of greater sophistication and greater profundity is not to begin to do justice to the difference between Zeus or Apollo and the God of Abraham and of Isaac and of Jacob, to say nothing of the God of the New Testament and of the Athanasian Creed. The difference between ancient Greek polytheism and Judaeo-Christian monotheism may be presented as not a mere difference in degree of complexity, or in stage of development along a single scale, but rather as a radical difference of kind, involving new dimensions that would be bound to defeat any attempt to relate that chalk to this cheese. The Christian gospel is *unique*, and Christian epistemology is therefore also *sui generis*.

I do not wish to minimize the differences between the doctrines of Christian theology and the very simple beliefs that I shall be examining. But the objection seems to me to exaggerate into an utter impossibility what is merely a difficulty, and a difficulty no greater than many that philosophers are accustomed to contend with. Moreover, that very difficulty can best be met by exactly the opposite policy from the one we shall be inclined to adopt if we take this objection too seriously. For in general the best way of understanding something that is complex and difficult is to set it beside something that is simpler and easier, something that we understand already or can more easily come to understand. And we shall find that even the simple cases present problems and difficulties that deserve attention. When we can understand and solve these problems we shall see more clearly the nature of the harder problems that lie ahead of us.

The simplest cases are linked with the most difficult by a continuous series of intermediate cases. There is an absolute continuity that connects ancient and primitive theology with contemporary sophisticated theology, a continuity unbroken by any jumps, gaps or sudden mutations. I am concerned here with a *logical* continuity, one that would still be visible even if there had been many sudden breaks and leaps in the actual historical development of religion and theology. But in fact there have been no such breaks or leaps. The historical continuity that can be traced from the Book of Genesis to the present day, or from Homer to the present day, serves to underline the logical continuity between the primitive and the more highly developed. Where there is such an unbroken historical development, there cannot be a logical gap or gulf.

This historical continuity and this logical continuity can both be seen again in the development of every individual Christian in his growth from a primitive and childish understanding of the affirmations of his faith, when he is a child, to a more advanced and sophisticated understanding of them, when he grows up and puts away childish things.

The importance of these continuities for my present inquiry is evident again in the overlappings and interconnections between Judaeo-Christian theology and Greek theology. In the Christian tradition we find not only St Augustine and St Thomas and Kierkegaard, but also Elijah and his tussle with the prophets of Baal. Among the Greeks we have the simple, primitive belief of Homer, but we also have the sophisticated metaphysical theology of Plato and Aristotle. There is the orthodox theology of Aeschylus or Sophocles, but there is also the modernist revisionary theology of Euripides. Even in very early Greek times, we find not only Homer's anthropomorphic pictures of the gods and goddesses, but also the trenchant attacks of Xenophanes upon all theological anthropomorphism.

Even when our eyes are fixed on the differences between the ancient and the modern, the simple and the complex – and I insist rather than deny that there are great differences as well as continuous connections – we must attend to cases of both kinds, we must understand both sides of the comparison or contrast, if we are to say to what extent and in what respect they differ. We do, after all, call these ancient gods *god*. Why do we call them gods? What are the patterns of analogy or family resemblance that link them with the God of Isaac under the same general term 'god'? If the differences had been of such a kind and on such a scale that there was no connection between God and the ancient gods, it would no longer be natural and correct to apply the same term at both ends of the scale.

A parallel case will illustrate further why I attach importance to the historical and logical continuity between ancient and modern theology. Life, including human life, has emerged from inanimate matter. There is a physical, historical continuity extending from the primeval slime to Shakespeare and Newton, and with this physical continuity there goes a logical continuity. Since, as a matter of historical fact, there was a gradual development from the primeval slime to Shakespeare, there cannot be a logical gap or discontinuity on the logical scale that connects Shakespeare with the primeval slime. And just as this does not involve denying that there are great and important differences between a person and a piece of inanimate matter, so when I emphasize the unbroken historical and logical continuities between ancient and modern theology I am not involved in denying that there are great and important differences between the two.

This is a field in which, as in the philosophy of religion, clarity can be served and puzzlement dispelled by an understanding of Wittgenstein's doctrine of family resemblances and Aristotle's logic of analogy. Disputes about whether machines could conceivably think, and in general about the nature of mind and personality and personal identity, are often bedevilled by just the assumption of a radical logical discontinuity that I wish to dispel from the discussion of the nature of theology. There is absolute continuity between a piece of mere machinery and a human being, in spite of the difference of kind between a person and an inanimate object. We must set out the differences concretely and in detail, and not imagine that there must be some specific element or essence that is present in the one case and absent in the other. The discipline of attention to cases, and especially to intermediate cases and to continuities between cases, is a defence against many philosophical confusions and mistakes.

For our detailed examples of ancient theology, let us turn first to the works of Homer. Let us suppose that Homer is resurrected, and that we are walking with him by the seashore on a stormy day. As we walk along the cliffs Homer may say to us: 'Poseidon is angry today.' And it would be quite natural for us to answer in the same terms, to say: 'Certainly, Poseidon is very angry today.' We both use the same words, 'Poseidon is angry'; and yet it is clear that there is a vast difference between what Homer is doing with these words and what we, with our much greater knowledge of meteorology and oceanography, are doing with the same words. One way of describing the difference would be to say that when Homer says that Poseidon is angry he is offering what is meant to be an *explanation* of the lashing of the waves, whereas when we say that Poseidon is angry we are giving no more than a picturesque *description* of the lashing of the waves. It is true that there is a profound connection between the explanation that Homer offers and the description that we offer. It is not an accident that we both use the same words for our different purposes. The features of a stormy sea that make the anger of a superhuman spirit a plausible explanation of its behaviour also make the picture of the anger of a superhuman spirit a natural means of describing the behaviour of the sea. And the description is an *accurate* description; it is not a *mere* metaphor or picture. There is something in the lashing of a stormy sea that is correctly described by saying that it is angry.

Neverthelesss, the difference between Homer and ourselves, in the scene that I have imagined, is of fundamental importance. One way of marking it would be to say that Homer has *expectations* that we lack. Even if he does not expect that he himself will ever see the god Poseidon appearing in person, on earth or on the surface of the waves, he has expectations that we do not have in the sense that he believes in the *existence* of such a being as Poseidon, independently of the waves that are his manifestations. And we must not be too sure that he would not have expected, in certain circumstances, to see the god himself, with his own mortal eyes.

Here we must remember the background against which Homer thinks and speaks of Poseidon. In hills that Homer has seen and trodden there are springs that were caused to spout forth by the stamp of Poseidon's hoof when he appeared in the guise of a horse. In Homer's audience there are descendants of Poseidon. In the history of himself and his own people there are events in which Poseidon has dramatically intervened. He knows men and women who have seen Poseidon, in visions, or in dreams, or even making personal appearances at critical junctures in their lives. We rightly claim to know that these expectations are unsatisfiable and therefore inappropriate, *mistaken* expectations. Our knowledge of meteorology and other sciences has weaned us from speaking of Poseidon as Homer spoke of him. We may still say: 'The wind bloweth where it listeth'; but we know too much about the world to use these words in the sense and in the spirit in which they were first used. The wind may still be called capricious; but we know that it is not really capricious in that full and strong sense in which some of our friends are capricious. And that it is not capricious in that sense is a matter of fact which might have been otherwise. It is by factual evidence that we establish that the wind is not subject to the whims of a spirit.

Similarly, Poseidon does not, as a matter of fact, exist; but it *is* a *fact* that he does not exist. It is a matter of empirical, contingent fact that the moods of the sea are not the moods of a superhuman spirit, Poseidon. And like any other matter of fact, it might have been otherwise. There might have been sufficient evidence *for* the existence of Poseidon instead of sufficient evidence against it. It might have been true that a superhuman spirit did control the winds and waves in the way in which Homer thought that Poseidon controlled them. But once we have come to believe – on the excellent grounds that we now have for believing it – that Poseidon does not in this sense exist, if we nevertheless continue to use the *words* 'Poseidon is angry', it must be something different that we mean by them.

At the end of our conversation with Homer he would rightly say, when he *found us out*, that we had only pretended to believe in Poseidon, that we did not really believe in Poseidon at all.

My second example also comes from Homer, and it is typical of many that are to be found in the *Iliad* and the *Odyssey*. When Telemachus was in trouble and needed advice and help, Athena appeared to him in the guise of his tutor, Mentor. Homer's description of this incident allows of several distinct interpretations, which must be distinguished as sharply and carefully as possible. The first possibility is that there are on the face of the earth at the time when Athena appears to Telemachus in the guise of Mentor *two* bodies of Mentor in different places. It may be that the real, ordinary Mentor is lying asleep in Mentor's bed, and that Athena puts on a different, *extra* 'body of Mentor' for the sake of her appearance before

Telemachus. A second possibility is that Athena may appear to Telemachus *in* the one, single, ordinary body of Mentor that is standing before Telemachus, while nevertheless it is not now *Mentor* but the superhuman Athena who inhabits and speaks through that body.

The third possibility is that it is *Mentor himself*, mind *and* body, who stands before Telemachus, and that the words that he speaks are his own words, and yet are inspired beyond the normal powers of Mentor, inspired by Athena, that is to say, by Athena as goddess of wisdom, that is to say, at the theoretical limit, by wisdom itself as an animistic abstraction.

It is true that at the end of the incident described by Homer, Telemachus recognizes that he has been in the presence of a god. But this element in the narrative has the same multiplicity as the rest of the description. It is compatible with any one of the three different interpretations that I have suggested.

Now the point I want to make about this example is that the first and second interpretations – namely (1) that according to which there are two Mentor bodies in different places, and (2) that according to which the superhuman spirit, Athena, is inside the one single body of Mentor – are both *false*; that they are, as a matter of *fact*, false; that they might have been true, but that we know too much about the world to be prepared to believe that they ever are true, that incidents of the kind described by Homer ever happen in such a sense that they must be described according to the first or the second interpretation.

According to the third interpretation, we are just as happy to speak of Athena appearing to Telemachus in the guise of Mentor as we were to speak of Poseidon causing the waves to be angry, and for the same reason. For the third interpretation is not one that can be allowed to count as or to constitute *really believing in Athena*. If Homer discovered that we accepted his description but insisted on interpreting it in the third way, he would again say, and would rightly say, that we no more believed in Athena than we believed in Poseidon.

The third example that I wish to consider has a wider range and scope, and it brings us much nearer to the problems about the nature and justification of Christian theology which I shall be discussing in later lectures. It concerns the similarities and

differences between the theological beliefs of the three great
Greek tragedians, Aeschylus, Sophocles and Euripides. In
Greek terms, Aeschylus and Sophocles are orthodox, conventional theologians. They tell stories in which the power of the
Greek gods is portrayed, together with the influence of those
gods on human life and conduct. In the stories of Agamemnon
and Prometheus and Oedipus they set before us dramatic
instances of the intervention of divine powers in human life,
and of the responses of human beings to such interventions.
Euripides tells the same stories, and vividly presents the same
aspects of human life and experience. In the *Hippolytus*, the
Bacchae, and the *Medea* we have the same mythological machinery, the same apparatus, put to a very similar use. Human
life is mirrored and portrayed by means of pictures of the same
deities engaged in the same interventions in human existence.
And yet even in his own time Euripides was thought to be an
atheist, and it is still an open question among scholars whether
he was indeed an atheist, or just a very modernistic theologian.
Once again we find that what makes a plausible explanation
also makes a good description. Aeschylus and Sophocles believed
that the gods and goddesses they wrote about were responsible
for, and could therefore be invoked to explain, the phenomena
of human life and experience. It is quite possible that Euripides
did not believe any such thing; but the vividness with which he
presents the same human experiences in the same theological
terms is not thereby reduced.

This point can be further strengthened. The same Greek
pantheon and the same Greek theology are often used by
modern writers for the same purpose of presenting and describing and commenting on exactly the same elements in the
experience that we share with the ancient Greeks. We all
have experience of the power of Aphrodite and of the contrary
power of Artemis. We have all witnessed conflicts between the
powers of destiny and chance and the feebler powers of human
choice. We all have experience of the arbitrariness and capri-
ciousness of the powers of nature and of human nature. We may
not agree with him, but Freud was speaking in a way that we
can understand, and in a way that any ancient Greek would
have understood, when he said that 'dark, unfeeling and
unloving powers control man's destiny'. Our world is sufficiently

like the world of Homer and Aeschylus and Sophocles for the stories that they tell in their theological terms to continue to be meaningful to us and valuable to us. Different as our world is in some ways, it is similar enough in other and perhaps profounder ways for the literature of the ancients, even when it is expressed through a theological apparatus that we have given up, to continue to have a powerful appeal to us and an abiding value for us.

But what mainly concerns us now is that we *have* given up their theological apparatus. Our experience is sufficiently different from theirs to change our relation to the basis of the stories that they tell. We do not believe in these gods; and we have good reasons for not believing in them. What was intended by Greek theologians as dogma, doctrine, truth, has become for us a manner of speaking, a mode of projection, reinterpreted and *demythologized*.

That last word raises all the questions about modern theology that have lain behind my remarks about the Greeks. Modern theologians and philosophers – Bonhoeffer, Bultmann, Tillich, Braithwaite and the Bishop of Woolwich – have done to traditional Christian words something as radical as we have done to the words of Homer and Sophocles. Have they done the *same* thing? Is their talk of God, like my talk of Poseidon and Athena, so different from what such talk used to be that it would be better, clearer, more honest, to find new words for expressing what is in effect a new belief?

The simple Greek examples not only raise these questions: they also suggest provisional answers to them. I propose that we try to be as clear as we can about the nature of these examples, and take their features as provisional guides to the nature of theology more generally, unless and until we see reason to abandon them.

The first lesson suggested by the Greek examples is that theology must be rooted in our world if we are to have any understanding of it and any ground for believing in it; that a theological doctrine cannot be relevant to the lives that we are called upon to live in this world unless it has something to say about the world in which we are called upon to live those lives. I am not here trying to break down the distinction between natural theology and revealed theology. Even revealed theology requires its points of contact with the ordinary, familiar world. A revelation must be mediated through a sacred book, or through the words of a prophet, or through the authoritative deliverances of a church. Revealed theology, just like natural theology, stands in need of outward criteria. It is by reading that book, by hearing the words of that prophet, by attending to the pronouncements of that church, that we are called upon to judge and to assess the meaning and the truth of the revelation.

The second lesson lies in the distinction that I drew between explanation and mere description. While the remarks of a theologian must be based on familiar or at least accessible facts and features of the world of our ordinary experience, they must also refer to something over and above the facts and features on which they are based. If the words of a theological formula are used merely as a pictorial re-description of the phenomena that they refer to, they cannot still be allowed to count as the expression of a genuine belief in what those who use those words are purporting to believe in.

Consider the application of my example of Athena and Telemachus to the doctrine of the Resurrection. Just as Homer would find out that we did not really believe in Athena at all, so, I suggest, we ought to hesitate, if not refuse, to say that some-body really believes in the Resurrection of Jesus Christ if he gives such an account of it that it no longer has or claims to have the grip on external, factual historical events that the doctrine had when it was propounded in its original and traditional form. Some recent writers have made such radically different uses of traditional words that they have implicitly abandoned the traditional doctrines that those words have traditionally been used to express. Some theologians, for example, have identified the Resurrection with the fact that the gospel of Christ continues to be preached – a version that makes believers of us all, but only in the sense in which we all believe in Homer's gods.

There are difficulties and dilemmas for theology here. When we trace the gradual modifications that have been made in the use of theological forms of words, we seem to find that we are faced with a choice between two alternatives which are both, though for different reasons, unpalatable and embarrassing to the traditional and orthodox believer. He may affirm the traditional doctrine in the sense that it has traditionally borne, but find that his affirmation when taken in that sense can be shown to be false; or he may affirm the doctrine in a sense in which it can readily be accepted as true, but in which it can no longer be identified with the original doctrine of which he is continuing to *say* that it is true. A theological doctrine must be attached to *our* world, must have *some* basis in our world, but it must also go beyond our world in such a sense that it will not be simply identifiable with, or reducible to, a mere description of the phenomena in our world which are offered as its basis or evidence.

In the case of each of the simple doctrines that we have so far considered it seems clear that there is no escape from the dilemma. Each of the doctrines satisfies these requirements only in a sense in which it is clearly false, and is true only in senses in which it does not satisfy these requirements.

The importance of these points for my wider purpose becomes clearer still if we think again of the programme of 'demytholog- ization' which has been so prominent in recent theology, and of reinterpretations of Christian theology, such as those offered by Matthew Arnold and Professor R. B. Braithwaite, from which all or most of the traditional doctrinal affirmations of the Christian Church have been explicitly deleted. It seems at least at first sight that there is an important parallel between what is done by Arnold or Bultmann or Braithwaite and what is done by Euripides, and that there is room for the same doubt in the case of Braithwaite or Bultmann or Arnold as there is in the case of Euripides: a doubt as to whether what is now being affirmed is what it purports to be; a suspicion that the use of traditional words has now been carried so far away from the original and basic use that an element of deception or at least of self- deception is involved in the use of the old words for the ex- pression of the new belief.

These issues come to a head in one particular but crucial issue that is raised for these radical innovators in theology and philosophy of religion by the traditional claim of the Christian religion to unique truth and validity. If we adopt a particular religion, but interpret its beliefs in such a way as to equate them with descriptions of familiar phenomena, or treat them as 'stories' whose truth value is regarded as irrelevant to their religious function, it is hard to see that we can press this process of demythologization very far before reaching a point where we can no longer be allowed to reject other religions as being incompatible with the particular religion that we wish to accept. There is no incompatibility between a refurbished, demythologized Homeric polytheism, a refurbished, demythologized Islam, and a refurbished, demythologized Christianity. When the words that have traditionally been used to express the doctrines of these religions come to be used in such a way that they express no more than the familiar facts on which the doctrines are held to be based as evidence, then we have entirely lost the incompatibility between one religion and another which must be maintained by orthodox Christianity and by any other religion which claims to be *the* true religion. Orthodoxy implies the possibility of heresy, just as heresy presupposes the existence of an orthodoxy.

Now there cannot be any application of the notions of orthodoxy or heresy to any field in which there is no application for the closely related and fundamentally important concepts of assertion, proposition, reason, justification, knowledge and ignorance, truth and falsehood, consistency and contradiction. The most important provisional lesson of my examination of some elementary theological beliefs is that these concepts, which some recent philosophers and theologians have been prepared to banish from theological inquiry, are as indispensable to theology as to any other sphere in which the human mind may seek for insight and understanding. This provisional conclusion cannot be withdrawn unless we find strong reasons for supposing that the more advanced theological doctrines that we have still not considered are radically different from these simple doctrines, and yet not so radically different as to cease to be *theological* doctrines at all.

3 · Labyrinth

My simple examples have turned out not to be so simple after all. The path from Mount Olympus to the labyrinth at the heart of the philosophy of theology is shorter and straighter than it seemed. We have soon reached our central questions: questions about faith and reason, about the relation between the will and the understanding, about the place in theology of the notions of assertion, belief, proposition and contradiction; questions, in fact, about the *logic* of theological inquiry, affirmation and belief.

It is not hard to see why the simple examples have led to the complex questions. They are the historical starting-point of the growth and development of western theology, and they are also the *logical* starting-point of theology, in the sense that they occupy one end of a scale of cases of theological belief which passes by continuous gradations to the most sophisticated and advanced varieties of theological assertion and commitment. But they do not belong only to a remote past or to an ideal limit on a philosopher's neatly diagrammatic scale. They retain a great contemporary interest and importance, as I can show by pursuing a hint that I gave in my preliminary comments on them.

These elementary beliefs are also elemental, fundamental. They are the starting-point for each one of us in his search for religious understanding. Everybody who believes in God, and nearly everybody who does not believe in God, has begun, as a child, by believing in a god as primitive and simple as the gods of the ancient Greeks. At his mother's knee, or at school or Sunday school, he has learnt to believe propositions which have the same logical character as the ancient Greek beliefs that I have described. And some people, for good or ill, remain as little children. It is not everybody who, when he becomes a man, puts away childish things. Every Christian congregation has its shepherds as well as its wise men. Even many unbelievers share a conception of the nature of religious belief which links them more closely with the ancient Greek theologians than with the sophisticated and advanced theologians of this or any age.

The same conception may be found again in the minds of many, whether believers or unbelievers, who would explicitly repudiate such an interpretation of the doctrines of Christian theology. It is not necessary that a man should openly recognize and acknowledge that he understands a particular form of words in a certain way in order for it to be true and evident that he understands it in that way. This point can be illustrated by two important examples from other fields in philosophy.

Plato and Descartes would explicitly and sincerely deny that they thought of the human mind or soul as having a spatial location, or as having any of the properties that characteristically belong to extended and material bodies. But the ways in which they elsewhere speak about the immaterial soul give strong ground for the suspicion that they do in fact sometimes, if not always, think of the soul as having material or quasi-material properties. They think of my soul or mind as having a relation to my body which it does not have to your body or to any other material thing. But they do not explain, and it is hard to see how they could explain, how an immaterial substance could have a relation to a particular material object that it did not have to any other material object.

An analogous point arises in connection with Plato's theory of transcendent Forms or universals. He would strenuously deny that he thought of the Forms as having a spatial location, but here again the language in which he speaks of them leaves no doubt that the picture of the Forms or universals as forming a quasi-material world, which transcends the familiar material world, is a picture that does operate in Plato's mind, and gives its character to his explicit philosophical account of the nature of universals. I suggest that similarly, in the minds of many who would explicitly and sincerely repudiate the simple theological pictures that I have been examining, such simple pictures are still powerfully influential.

All this underlines the importance of the simple pictures, and helps to indicate the role that they fulfil in my wider investigation. It is from such pictures that the sophisticated theologian departs, and by reference to them that his doctrines are to be understood. The forms of words that he uses have as their primary use the expression of these elementary beliefs, and it is only when these elementary beliefs are recognized to be false that their forms of expression are put to new uses. If we are clear about the nature of the beliefs expressed by these forms of words in their primary use we shall be able to follow step by step their gradual conversion to new uses and to assess their fitness or unfitness for their new tasks; to see whether they retain enough or lose too much of their original purpose and import to be recognizable still as expressions of the doctrines they once expressed or indeed as expressions of any theological doctrines at all.

The adoption of this procedure does not imply that nothing can be a theological doctrine unless it closely conforms to the simple primary examples, but it ensures as far as possible that we shall not allow superficial resemblances to conceal from us more fundamental differences. The simple examples are not functioning as paradigms to which all examples must conform on pain of exclusion, but as points of reference which will help us to distinguish internal variations within the range of theological beliefs from differences that cross the boundaries of the range. We shall be prepared, but only for strong reasons, to recognize cases of theological belief that are widely different from the primary examples; and the strong reasons must take the form of links of analogy or resemblance that count for more than the important differences. We shall be particularly reluctant to give up any of the three leading features of the primary examples: (1) that they are all clearly cases of *assertions* and of assertions of *fact*; (2) that each of them rests on a basis in our world, in the familiar world that is open and accessible to all of us; and that this applies to those that are held to be based on revelation as well as to those that are supported directly by reference to features of our ordinary experience; (3) that each makes a claim not only to the effect that those features of the world which are cited in its support *are* features of the world, but also to the effect that something over and above those features exists and can be known.

It is time to leave these comfortable simplicities and to move to the more dangerous and difficult stage of examining the further implications of the character of the examples that I have

described. We shall need to attend to fine distinctions and to
subtle differences between one use and another of the same
form of words. We have seen that even in the simple case of
Mentor and Telemachus some fine distinctions may be dis-
cerned, and they are a sample of the gradations by which the
more simple evolves into the more complex. It is in these trans-
itions, pregnant with revolution but disguised by conservatism
in the uses of the forms of words that they underlie, that the
greatest perplexities lurk both for the religious inquirer and for
the philosopher of religious inquiry.

We shall meet these perplexities face to face if we look again
at the parallel that I have drawn between the historical development of western theology as a whole and the individual
development of each individual believer or unbeliever. Questions that were faced by Plato or Euripides or Xenophanes or
Protagoras are questions that we have all had to face for ourselves if we were instructed in our early years in the elements of
the Christian religion.

We are all familiar, either in our own experience or in the
experience of others, with the situation of a man who has
accepted in his early youth a theological doctrine about the
nature of the world and life and then finds that that doctrine is
too simple and too narrow and too literal to face up to a widen-
ing experience and a growing knowledge. And this is the
position that Xenophanes and Euripides and Protagoras and
Plato found themselves in. They found that they could not
continue to use old forms of words in the ways in which they
had been used by their original authors; and then, like modern
men in a similar predicament, they had to choose between two
alternative responses to it. They could conclude that because the
simple formulations had turned out to be false when understood in the simple and literal ways in which they had been
intended, they were simply and straightforwardly false, and
must be rejected – as *we* now reject Homer's beliefs about
Poseidon and Athena. This is the conclusion to which Protagoras was drawn, and it is the conclusion to which many in our
own day – Bertrand Russell, Fred Hoyle, Antony Flew –
have been drawn.

The alternative reaction is to say: 'Yes, indeed these formulations are false in the simple senses in which they were originally

D

meant to be taken, but we must not take them in their original and literal senses. If they are understood in another and deeper sense, they are true: they are *essentially* true, they are true when they are properly understood.' This was the reaction of Xenophanes, of Plato and possibly of Euripides. For many centuries, and until very recent times, it continued to be the reaction of most theologians and of many philosophers of religion.

Both these responses have been made again and again in every age, including our own, in which there has been theological debate and doubt and difficulty. To discuss them is at once to be involved in the current controversies about demythologization and about images of God, about Bultmann and the Bishop of Woolwich; but it is also to see these controversies in a wider historical perspective.

Neither of the two responses is satisfactory unless it is accompanied by an examination of the alternative senses that those who choose the second response can offer in place of the literal meanings which both parties agree to reject. If the debate is to be continued after the literal assertions of primitive theology have been given up, we must have detailed notice of the changes that are being made in the uses of the old theological expressions. The first response will be inadequate if it straitjackets the notions of fact and of assertion by suggesting that nothing which is not a straightforward, literal, factual assertion is a factual assertion at all, and if it does not pause to consider what legitimate alternative uses there may be for the sentences whose literal claims it wishes to reject.

The second way, which does recognize that there may be new dimensions of meaning, over and above the simple and the literal, in the use of traditional forms of words, must go further than this recognition. It must tell us, specifically, what use it now intends to make of those forms of words, so as to make plain to us what it is asserting as well as what it is denying. We must be told either what factual meaning the old formulae convey when they no longer convey their literal factual meaning, or what *non-factual* meaning they can bear which will nevertheless maintain them in a sufficiently close connection with their original factual meaning to preserve their status as expressions of *theological* doctrines.

The suggestion that theological utterances are significant but non-factual, that theological assertions are not *assertions*, raises separate issues and will be considered later. In this lecture I am concerned only with those responses in which a recognition of the propositional, indicative character of theology, or at any rate of its central pronouncements, is preserved.

The first and simplest version of the view that theological propositions are factual but are not to be understood in their traditional literal senses may be quickly dismissed, since I have already, by implication, offered conclusive reasons against it. One response to the predicament I have described is to say that theological propositions, though they are not literally true, are nevertheless straightforward factual claims about the natural world, since they are to be understood as restatements of the evidence that is produced in support of them. According to this view, which, by analogy with similar doctrines in other fields of philosophy, may be called 'reductionism', theological propositions of the simple kind that I have discussed, whether Christian or pagan, are pictorial summaries of simple and familiar facts of our experience. But this view involves such gross equivocation between one use and another of the same theological form of words that anybody who maintains it must be suspected at least of confusion and at the worst of dishonesty. It simply will not do to say, for example, that Poseidon does truly exist, but that his existence merely consists in the fact that the wind and the waves and the weather behave in certain familiar ways. The believer in Poseidon offers *evidence* for a *conclusion*, and a relation between one proposition and another is a relation between evidence and conclusion only when the conclusion *is* another and distinct proposition that goes beyond the evidence, that says something that is not said in a statement or restatement of the evidence.

A second and far more considerable attempt to defend the factuality of theological assertions, and hence their capacity to be true-or-false, while nevertheless recognizing that in their most literal forms they are *plainly* false, is made by the kind of view according to which the truth or falsehood of theological propositions is a matter of faith or will or choice rather than a matter of reason or evidence. This type of view preserves the recognition that there is an objectively right answer to a theological question – for example, to the question 'Does God exist?' – but it suggests that it is necessarily useless for us to try to *discover* by any form of argument or reasoning or investigation whether a particular theological proposition that may be offered in answer to such a question is in fact true or false. Under this heading is to be found the heretical doctrine known as *fideism*, the doctrine that faith alone determines whether a man recognizes or fails to recognize the truth of a doctrine which is nevertheless an objectively *true* doctrine, independently of being believed or recognized to be true. This category also includes various forms of self-avowed *irrationalism*, ranging from Tertullian's *certum quia impossibile* to Tillich's insistence that *every* belief, and not just every theological belief, ultimately rests on an arbitrary commitment.

It is clear already that there is great internal variety within this category of responses, and in another context or for another purpose it would be necessary to consider in detail each of the main specimens of the species. But the species as a whole suffers from an epistemological disease that is fatal to every specimen, and I shall here confine myself to the diagnosis of that disease and some remarks on its pathology.

The aetiology of the disease can be understood by looking again at the predicament that evokes this type of view. One who has been deeply convinced of the truth of a theological doctrine, but who has come to recognize that an impartial assessment of the evidence shows that the doctrine is false, may naturally seek some way of avoiding *both* the abandonment of his faith *and* such a radical reinterpretation of it as would constitute the abandonment of the traditional form of it to which he has been committed. He may think that he has found such a way if he now declares that the consideration of reason and evidence is altogether irrelevant to questions about the truth or falsehood of his faith. He cannot lose a battle that is never joined or a game that he declines to play. And he will feel more comfortable as a mere spectator and non-combatant if he can suggest that he and his fellow theologians are not alone behind the sidelines, that there are other important questions besides those about God that are in principle unamenable to rational discussion and determination. He may reassure himself by incantations to the effect that, after all, science itself rests on an arbitrary and indefensible faith in the uniformity of nature, and pure mathematics on unprovable axioms and postulates. His self-confidence may grow to the proportions of an arrogance if he can persuade himself that he is licensed to cry '*tu quoque*' to all inquirers in all inquiries, because even the law of non-contradiction and the other 'laws of thought' are themselves arbitrarily adopted, so that he may at his discretion either take them or leave them.

There is certainly no reason why he should feel lonely. His reflections on the basis or baselessness of all human knowledge place him in the distinguished company of most of the philosophers of most ages. Bradley is a spokesman not only for Absolute Idealists when he writes:

> We are fastened to a chain, and we wish to know if we are really secure. What ought we to do? Is it of much use to say, 'This link we are tied to is certainly solid, and it is fast to the next, which seems very strong and holds firmly to the next; beyond this we can not see more than a certain moderate distance, but, so far as we know, it all hangs together?' The practical man would first of all ask, 'Where can I find the last link of my chain? When I know that it is fast, and not hung in the air, it is time enough to inspect the connection.' But the chain is such that every link begets, as soon as we come to it, a new one; and, ascending in our search, at each remove we are no nearer the last link of all, on which everything depends. The series of phenomena is so infected with relativity, that, while it is itself, it can never be made absolute. Its existence refers itself to what is beyond, and, did it not do so, it would cease to exist. A last fact, a final link, is not merely a thing which we cannot know, but a thing which could not possibly be real. Our chain by its nature cannot have a support. Its essence excludes a fastening at the end. We do not merely fear that it hangs in the air, but we know it must be so. And when the end is unsupported, all the rest is unsupported.
>
> *Principles of Logic* (1922), p. 100

It is a commonplace of philosophy that no proposition can be proved if it rests on any premise that cannot be proved, and also that every proposition rests ultimately on premises that cannot be proved, and hence that *no* proposition can ever be proved. But it involves misunderstandings that are as profound as the range of their application is wide.

These misunderstandings have a specially treacherous attraction for theologians and philosophers of religion. Difficulties about the nature of theological reasoning and difficulties in presenting reasons for particular theological doctrines may both, when they become acute, make it tempting to seek sanctuary in the feeling that here it is not necessary to present reasons for the very strong reason that it is not possible to present reasons. Theology, it is said, together with a good deal else that men have argued and debated and disputed about, is if rightly understood seen to be 'beyond argument', to lie outside the scope and competence of human reason.

Professor C. S. Lewis speaks in similar terms when he refers to his well-known disagreement with Dr Leavis about Milton and *Paradise Lost*:

> Dr Leavis does not differ from me about the properties of Milton's epic verse. He describes them very accurately – and understands them better, in my opinion, than Mr Pearsall Smith. It is not that he and I see different things when we look at *Paradise Lost*. He sees and hates the very same that I see and love. Hence the disagreement between us tends to escape from the realm of literary criticism.
>
> *A Preface to Paradise Lost*, p. 134

Lewis does not make clear whether he thinks that this puts the whole dispute between himself and Leavis 'beyond argument', but the dispute as he presents it is of just the kind that easily tempts philosophers, critics and theologians to describe it in this way. Whatever his own opinion may be on a point that he does not explicitly consider, I wish to express with emphasis and to defend with vigour the view that neither this nor any other question that can be at issue between two thinkers or writers or speakers is ever beyond the scope of reason.

Neither piety nor unbelief could ever give good grounds for the irrationalism which infects so many partisans of all parties in so many theological disputes. Neither in theology nor anywhere else is there any question which is, in the parrot-phrase of the irrationalists, 'beyond argument'. Wherever there is a question, there is scope for reasoning; wherever there is a dispute, there is something to be said that is relevant to the determination of that dispute. There is always scope for argument wherever there is disagreement – however many of us, on however many occasions, are either too impatient or too slow-witted or too wilful and dogmatic to be prepared or equipped to go on with the argument. Theology is a branch of *knowledge*; and it differs from other branches of knowledge – physics, mathematics, history, philosophy, morality – neither to a greater extent nor more fundamentally than they differ from each other. We know that the gods of Homer do not exist. And if we do not know whether the God of Abraham and of Athanasius exists, that is not because it is logically impossible that we should ever know. *There is work to be done.*

It follows that if God does not exist it would – with due respect to Voltaire – be crime and treason to invent him. And the crime would be a crime against Reason; the treason would be treason against Truth.

Even those who explicitly deny all this give it an implicit assent by the very fact that they persist in inquiry and dispute about the questions on which, according to their theory, inquiry and dispute are necessarily useless or even impossible. Their practice is better than their theory, and from their practice we can extract all the ingredients of a refutation of their theory. To extract these ingredients and to present this refutation will involve me in some amplification and revision of some of the results of recent general metaphysics and epistemology that I wish to apply to the study of philosophical theology, and in particular in setting out some of the logical relations between what might be called the *epistemic* concepts – concepts that have to do with knowledge, truth and reason.

Wherever there is a dispute or disagreement there is a question to which the parties to the dispute are offering different answers. Wherever there is a question there must clearly be the possibility of judgements and propositions which are possible answers to that question. Nothing can be an intelligible question at all unless it is possible to say of some judgements and propositions that they are answers to it, even if it is clear to us that the only answers we happen to be able to suggest are *wrong* answers, or such that we have no idea whether they are right or wrong. (But if they *are* answers they will be *either* right *or* wrong – not both and not neither.) A question may be understood as an invitation from the questioner to the auditor to say of a number of propositions, any one of which would be a possible, a *relevant* answer to the question, which are true and which are false. A question is an invitation to choose from among the range of propositions that are the relevant answers to that question.

Now wherever there are propositions and judgements there is also scope for contradiction. Every judgement or proposition has a contradictory which is also a judgement or proposition, and the range of propositions from among which a questioner is inviting us to choose will contain propositions which are incompatible with others that are contained in the same range. In fact the range will contain the contradictory of every proposition that it contains, since if a proposition is a relevant answer to a given question, the contradictory of that proposition is a relevant answer to the same question.

There is a sense of 'different answer' in which two people may give different answers to a question without being involved in any conflict or dispute. If somebody asks 'How tall is John?' and I say 'Six feet four inches' and you say 'Well over six feet' there need be no conflict between us. When I say that wherever there is a dispute there is a question to which the disputants are giving different answers I mean 'different answers' in the sense of *incompatible* answers, answers whose conjunction is self-contradictory.

Wherever there is contradiction, there is also truth and falsehood. A contradiction consists of a pair or set of propositions such that they cannot all be true. They can all be false, as in the case where you say that John is five feet tall and I say that he is six feet tall and he is in fact five feet six inches tall. But in the case where they are all false their contradictories are all true. It necessarily cannot be the case that they are all neither-true-nor-false. There can be a contradiction between my answer and your answer only if each answer is either true or false, since there can be a contradiction only if *either* (*a*) one of the two answers is true and the other false *or* (*b*) both answers are false.

Wherever there is truth and falsehood, there is scope for reasoning, understanding and knowledge. That this is so can be shown by examining the relations, much discussed but still much misrepresented, between meaning and verification or justification. The positivist mistake of identifying the meaning of a statement with its mode of verification was, like many if not most philosophical mistakes, an *understandable* mistake; not a *mere* mistake, but a misrepresentation of a logical point which deserves attention and can be re-stated without its disfiguring disguise. Meaning is not identical with verification, but meaning *involves* verification: there is no meaning where there is no mode of verification. To understand a statement is to have some idea of what would have to be the case for that statement to be true, and therefore to have some idea of what steps must be taken to find out whether it is true. To understand a question is to have some idea of what would count as an answer to it, and some idea of the steps by which it could be established for any given answer whether that answer is or is not a correct answer to it. Every unsettled question is at least a *settleable* question, an *arguable* question, for each party to a dispute about it is required to offer grounds for his answer. The difference between a certain answer's being true and its being false will always show itself in some other difference that makes that difference.

Irrationalists speak too glibly of 'agreeing to differ', and of absolute or fundamental disagreement. No disagreement *can* be absolute, since two parties cannot disagree about a question without agreeing on some other questions. Their disagreement is then over which of two alternative answers to the disputed question coheres better with their agreed answers to questions that are not in dispute. It is a great virtue of the much maligned 'coherence theory of truth' – to which I shall return in a later lecture – that it emphasizes this point about the nature of inquiry and dispute.

I recognize that I have been travelling in a circle in my exploration of these epistemic concepts: question, proposition, contradiction, truth and falsehood, reason and knowledge. But there is no circle in my argument against irrationalism. The irrationalist sees that some of these epistemic concepts apply to the inquiries of which he says that they are not rationally determinable. I am pointing out to him that the application of those concepts brings with it the application of the other epistemic concepts which according to him are not applicable to those inquiries.

I am suggesting that not only all theological questions, but all questions whatsoever, have right answers; that not only all unsettled theological questions, but all unsettled questions, are settleable and therefore arguable. And my thesis that every question has a right answer turns out, when placed in its setting among the epistemic concepts, to involve little if anything more exciting or more contentious than the text-book platitude that every proposition is either true or false but not both.

These considerations are of vast generality, but while they apply to much else, they do also apply to theology, and perhaps apply to it with special force because it is a field in which irrationalism is specially tempting. We find the same pattern repeated when we look at the concept of *transcendence*, which, either under its own name or in the guise of the *supernatural*, plays a prominent role in many responses to the predicament presented by the incipient sophistication of theology. The use of this concept is often associated with a resort to the fideist and irrationalist expedients that I have just been discussing, and there are logical links between these developments that must be explained in due course. But first it is necessary to outline the nature of transcendence in relative isolation from this background.

Here again the *Iliad* and the *Odyssey* are useful points of departure. In the *Iliad* the gods are represented as living on Mount Olympus – on the summit of an actual physical mountain whose lower slopes are familiar and easily accessible to Homer and his hearers. In the *Odyssey*, which is later – and perhaps belongs to a time when Mount Olympus had been climbed and found to be inhabited not by Zeus but only by his eagles – the Olympus of the gods is placed in the sky above all mountains. Once again we witness a gradual progression. By slow steps we come to an ethereal region, to those dwellings of the gods

> quas neque concutiunt venti nec nubila nimbis
> aspergunt neque nix acri concreta pruina
> cana cadens violat . . .
>   Lucretius III, 19–21

There is a parallel development in the conception of the gods themselves. Homer's assertions, although they refer to something over and above their own evidence, do not at first refer to anything outside and beyond his own familiar world. His gods and their heaven are part of the furniture of *this world*. Under the impact of a growing knowledge of the material world they are moved to a remoter region in physical space. But the pressures grow stronger. The move to the transcendent and the supernatural is made when it is suggested that facts about this world are evidence for the existence of beings in *another world*, when the gods are no longer spatially 'up there', but metaphysically 'out there'.

This move to the supernatural provides an appealing solution to the dilemma that I have discussed. A belief in a transcendent God is still a belief in the *existence* of something beyond the phenomena that are adduced as evidence in favour of the belief – it escapes the charge of reducing itself to a mere description – while it also contrives to escape the fate that Homer's primitive beliefs have suffered at the hands of our growing knowledge of the sciences. The sciences are concerned with this natural world, and God has now been placed in another world beyond their reach.

But the concept of the transcendent is involved in difficulties of its own; and these difficulties have become acute in recent times. For many centuries a belief in a transcendent God was in the distinguished company of a belief in transcendent material substances, transcendent minds, transcendent values, transcendent universals or Platonic Forms. In these other realms the rule of the transcendent has been at least gravely threatened, and possibly overthrown, by the insights and the arguments of metaphysicians and theorists of knowledge.

I cannot give here and now a general account of the steps by which I think it can be shown that in all these other fields a belief in transcendent entities has arisen from a misunderstanding of the nature of knowledge and its ultimate grounds. What I can do – though all too briefly – is to indicate the bearing of these wider issues on the doctrine of the transcendence of God. The main problem is this: how do we *know* that there are transcendent beings? What is the nature of the inference from statements about this world to statements about another world?

Transcendent objects seem to be so sharply distinguished from natural objects that it is hard to see how we can make the kind of connection between them that is required if we are to argue from facts about the one to conclusions about the other – and hard to see, therefore, how theological conclusions expressed in a transcendentalist idiom can remain rooted in the world in which we find ourselves.

The transcendentalist theologian is tempted to buy his immunity from refutation at the exorbitant price of a total failure to say anything about the world we know. It seems to make no difference to anything in our world whether his God exists or not.

A parallel from ethics and aesthetics may be useful here. I cannot say that there is no difference between two pictures except that one of them is beautiful and the other is not, or that one of them is ugly and the other is not. A claim that a picture has or lacks a certain aesthetic quality has to be supported by pointing out that it has or lacks certain other, non-aesthetic qualities. The same applies to the moral qualities of people and their characters and actions.

I suggest that the same point again applies to theology; and it can be very sharply put by asking the question: Is it conceivable that God should exist, and yet that everything else should remain exactly the same as if he did not exist? Is it conceivable that God should not exist, and yet that everything else should remain exactly the same as if he did exist?

It seems to me that transcendentalist theology has given no adequate answer to this challenge, and that it is a challenge which must be pressed with a particular urgency on Christian transcendentalists, since Christianity is a *historical* religion, a religion whose supreme article of faith is the Incarnation, the intersection of the timeless with time.

If transcendentalist theologians did give an adequate answer to this challenge, it is clear that they would still be meaning by their theological forms of words something radically different from what was originally meant. It is a consequence of the intimacy of the link between meaning and verification that where there is a radical change in mode of verification there is also a radical change in meaning. The fideist and the voluntarist altogether detach their theological affirmations from the facts of experience that were once the evidence for those affirmations, and so come to mean by them something substantially different from what was originally meant. The transcendentalist or supernaturalist continues to refer to the facts of experience, and to purport to use them as evidence for his supernaturalist conclusion. But the meaning of his conclusion is so different from that of the doctrine that was at first expressed in the same form of words that the mode of verification is substantially changed, and the facts of experience do not continue to bear the original simple inductive relation to the theological conclusion, but a new relation so mysterious and obscure that it is unclear whether it qualifies as a relation of evidential support at all.

In theology, as elsewhere, where there is transcendentalism there will also be scepticism. Theological scepticism consists in holding that while there is an objectively right answer to every theological question, one that is independent of anybody's faith or choice or wish, such questions are nevertheless in principle undecidable. Such scepticism is one of the two very different things that have sometimes been confused together under the label of agnosticism. Agnosticism properly so called is a *theological* view and not a metaphysical one. The agnostic maintains that it is *as a matter of fact* impossible for us to determine the truth or falsehood of particular theological propositions, or even the still weaker thesis that we have simply so far failed, though we might well have succeeded, in our efforts to verify or falsify certain theological propositions. What I am calling scepticism is the much more radical view that it is in principle impossible for us or for any beings constituted like ourselves to determine the truth or falsehood of theological doctrines.

This sceptical view is so closely akin to the irrationalist and fideist views that I have described that it is clearly open to very similar objections. The sceptic attributes meanings and truth-values to theological propositions but denies that they have verification-procedures. He thus contradicts not only the incorrect, positivist account which identifies meaning with verification, but also the truth that underlies the positivist mistake, that meaning and understanding *involve* verification; that there cannot be a question before us, we cannot be engaged in a dispute, unless we have some grasp of what would count for and against each of the views between which we are trying to adjudicate.

Scepticism, positivism, fideism, irrationalism and transcendentalism are a widely varied and mutually hostile group of doctrines. Each is in conflict at some important points with each of the others. But there are links between them, and an examination of these links is what will help us most in the next stage of our inquiry into the logic of theology. They have in common not only the challenge and the dilemma to which they are all trying to respond, but also, beneath all their striking idiosyncrasies, a kinship in the manner and substance of their response. They all begin by recognizing that many of the most characteristic theological doctrines are not simple assertions of straightforward fact. They all proceed to exaggerate the importance and to misconstrue the significance of this observation. They oversimplify and overdramatize the differences between primitive theology and developed theology, and ignore or misconceive the continuities that link them. They overlook the possibility that something which is not a simple or straightforward account of our familiar world may nevertheless be an account of our familiar world, and so conclude that when theology loses its simplicity and its straightforwardness it must also lose its contact with this world, and hence also its meaning, or its verifiability, or its rationality and objectivity.

What we need is an account which will preserve the recognition that theology is a search for *knowledge*, which will not obscure or deny the fact that some theological assertions are *true* and others *false*, but which will also do justice to complexities in the notions of fact and of theology which are misrepresented in the accounts I have so far examined. A sustained attempt to meet these requirements has been made by Professor John Wisdom in his celebrated paper on 'Gods' and in a number of more recent articles in which he elaborates and supplements its arguments. In my next lecture I will explain why I believe that Wisdom's account is an outstandingly important contribution to the philosophy of theology and yet that its high promise outruns its performance, so that it leaves unresolved some of the most bewildering of the perplexities with which it is concerned.

4 · Patterns

If the doctrines of ancient Greek theology are understood as simple propositions about straightforward matters of fact, then they are false. If the main doctrines of Christian theology are understood as simple propositions about straightforward matters of fact, then they too are false. It is widely agreed that the propositions of ancient Greek theology are to be understood in this way, and therefore it is widely agreed that they are false.

It would be possible in the case of Greek theology, and is usual in the case of Christian theology, for the debate to continue beyond this stage. To recognize that a particular theological doctrine is false if understood as a simple proposition of fact is not to be committed to rejecting or dismissing it. There are alternative interpretations that can be given both to the propositions of ancient Greek theology and to the propositions of Christian theology.

There are two different lines along which the debate can continue. It may be suggested that these theological propositions are factual, but are not simply and straightforwardly factual; or it may be suggested that theological doctrines do not express or even purport to express factual propositions at all, that their outward form is a misleading guide to their meaning and purpose.

I have considered several varieties of the first of these two approaches, and have given reasons for rejecting three widely favoured instances of this type of view: (1) the suggestion that theological propositions are to be understood as mere summaries of the natural facts to which, on other accounts, they are related as conclusions to evidence; (2) the view that they are verified by appeal to the eye of a faith that does not need to refer to reason or evidence at all; and (3) the species of agnosticism which maintains not simply that we do not and cannot as a matter of fact know whether theological propositions are true or false, but that it is in principle impossible for us or for any beings constituted as we are to know whether they are true or false.

This category also includes an approach which offers a greater promise of doing justice to the factual character of theological inquiry without yielding the conclusion that the most characteristic doctrines of orthodox Christianity are plain falsehoods about straightforward matters of fact. An account on these lines is developed in the writings of Professor John Wisdom to which I have already briefly referred. It is an application to the philosophy of theology of the descriptive and comparative method that I outlined in my first lecture. It has the great merit, which it shares with the wider philosophical theory in which it is set, of looking at theology, and at the other studies and inquiries with which it compares and contrasts theology, in all their untidiness and complexity and not trimmed to fit any preconceived blueprint for knowledge.

Though Wisdom proceeds by direct description and comparison of the instances and modes of thought with which he is concerned, and seldom engages in explicit polemic, his writings on the philosophy of religion amount to a reasoned rejection both of a number of traditional accounts of the nature of theology and of recent positivistic accounts. And the substance of his important contribution can be restated in the form of a frontal attack on the central assumptions of positivists, from Hume to Ayer, about meaning, reason, fact and knowledge.

Hume was prepared to commit to the flames 'any volume of divinity or school metaphysics' that did not contain either 'abstract reasoning concerning quantity or number' or 'experimental reasoning concerning matters of fact and existence'. He is the progenitor and patron of a long line of empiricist philosophers who have relished the havoc that, once 'persuaded of these principles', they have felt entitled to make in our libraries. Professor Ayer, riding high in *Language, Truth and Logic* on a verification principle or meaning-criterion that he himself described as a slightly less rhetorical version of Hume's doctrine, gave theologians the cold comfort of an assurance that their agnostic and atheist opponents shared the misfortune of being concerned with questions and statements which were devoid of literal significance.

Ayer was right in supposing that his principles required the abandonment of theology to a limbo outside the scope of positive knowledge and significant inquiry. Theology is neither a natural science nor a branch of pure mathematics or formal logic, and it necessarily fails to satisfy a blueprint which makes those inquiries not merely the paradigms but the sole exemplars of rational discourse.

The havoc was not confined to the divinity and metaphysics shelves of our libraries. The consequences of the positivist doctrine were so pervasive that if its ruthless consistency had been a little more consistent it would have been very much more ruthless. For the paradigms of logic and science that the positivists used as bludgeons against other inquiries were too crude to serve even as paradigms of logic and science. If their programme had been strictly carried out they would have been forced to commit to the flames many books, including their own, that they wished to preserve from the holocaust.

Most of Wisdom's work, inside and outside the philosophy of religion, has been directed against such restrictive schematizations, and in particular against the Humean and positivist schema according to which all reasoning follows the relatively simple and memorable patterns of deduction and induction that are described by logicians in their text-books. He maintains not only that there are modes of valid reasoning which are neither deductive nor inductive, but also, and more radically, that deductive and inductive reasoning themselves ultimately depend on modes of reasoning which are neither inductive nor deductive. He suggests that the ultimate forms of reasoning in all fields of inquiry fail to fit the text-book patterns of deduction and induction, and that therefore it is small wonder that those who are blinkered by the positivist dichotomy should oscillate between a scepticism to which they are driven when they recognize that the ultimate grounds of all our reasonings are neither deductive nor inductive, and manifold forms of mis-representation of all our modes of reasoning to which they are impelled when they find scepticism intolerable.

Theology has repeatedly suffered at the hands of philosophers whose chief implement was Hume's fork. Any attempt to give strict criteria for separating out genuine reasoning from what is not reasoning at all, and especially one which uses deduction

E

and induction as its twin paradigms, is bound to lead to distortion and misdescription of theological reasoning in one way or another. Either theology will be mis-shaped by being pressed into the deductive or the inductive mould, or it will be misrepresented as not being a genuine mode of reasoning, and will accordingly be rejected altogether, because it fails to fit into either of these moulds. Philosophers who try to defend theology by misdescribing it as quasi-scientific or quasi-logical and philosophers who attack theology because they recognize that it is neither quasi-scientific nor quasi-logical have been led to their equal and opposite mistakes by a third mistake in which they disastrously agree. They have failed to recognize the existence and the importance of kinds of reasoning which are *a priori* but non-deductive, of logical connections which are *a priori* but non-necessary. They have ignored the central role inside and outside philosophy of the kind of reasoning in which, in Wisdom's phrase, the premises support the conclusion 'not like the links of a chain, but like the legs of a chair'.

In an article on Existentialism Wisdom applies these points to the ancient search for the essence of the good life, for a formula expressing the nature of the *summum bonum*:

> The Existentialist is represented as answering with a string of negations 'not the promotion of what belongs in the field of my professional duties; not wife, children and friends; not wealth, learning or power; not higher living standards for all men; not . . .'
>
> Suppose it is true that no one of these things is sufficient to make life meaningful. It does not follow that life is not meaningful. Suppose further that it is true that no one of these things is necessary to life's having a meaning. It does not follow that life hasn't a meaning nor even that it isn't these things which give it its meaning. After all no one of a horse's legs suffices to keep him standing up, and at the blacksmith's it is demonstrated that no leg is indispensable for his standing up, but of course this doesn't mean that no horse stands up nor that he stands up on anything but his own legs. To win a set at tennis is not the *summum bonum* but this doesn't prove that it is not *part* of what makes *a* life good.

Paradox and Discovery, pp. 36-7

When he brings these and similar examples to bear on theology, Wisdom is led to use analogies and to make comparisons which have been neglected by those who were tethered to the paradigms of mathematics and physics. Though he begins, like the positivists and Professor Braithwaite, by contrasting theological propositions with propositions of mathematics and propositions of empirical science, he goes on to *compare* theology with modes of cognition and comprehension which are also misrepresented by positivistic accounts, but which we are much more reluctant than in the case of theology to abandon as irrational or to remould into the deductive and inductive patterns to which the positivists wish to restrict us. His chief examples are cases of moral reasoning, legal reasoning and aesthetic reasoning. He emphasizes the frequency and the importance in each of these fields of occasions when we can achieve and convey knowledge and understanding by seeing and showing a pattern of relationships between a set of items in which each separate item is already available for inspection, where no item is hidden and no further *data* are called for, and where nevertheless the process of exhibiting the pattern is not one of performing formal deductive transformations of the existing data or premises.

Here as usual the besetting sin of philosophers has been a craving for unity, simplicity and generality. They have supposed that all knowing and seeing and recognizing must be of one, or of one or two, simple and straightforwardly describable varieties. They have therefore overlooked or misrepresented the cases in which we gain new knowledge by informal reflection on facts that are already available to us.

Many such cases are simple and trivial enough to be elementary and therefore fundamental, to be the solid rock of common knowledge and common understanding in which the skyscrapers of the special arts and sciences are grounded. Many others call for powers of insight or understanding which, for all their informality and their stubborn resistance to attempts to subject them to any formal and general rules, are as sophisticated and advanced as the techniques of any specialist.

If an illiterate child and a learned professor look at the same page of print, there is a clear sense in which they are both looking at the same thing. But there is an equally clear and equally important sense in which they see quite different things. An art critic and an untutored layman may both be looking at the same impressionist painting, and may yet see very different things. An antique dealer may see at a glance a vast difference between two pieces of silver which are to me indistinguishable.

I am not here concerned only or mainly with the more recondite properties which the skill of the reader or critic or dealer equips him to see in the page or the picture or the pieces of plate. The experts can of course, as the layman cannot, identify Petrarchan sonnets and early Rembrandts, or distinguish a piece of Georgian silver from a well-made copy of the same piece of Georgian silver. My present point is that the experts can do these things only because they can, in a much more elementary sense of 'see', *see* things that are missed by those who lack their training and experience.

The layman who has until now seen only directly representational, naturalistic pictures may fail to see that the impressionist painting that is now before him is a representational painting at all; he may insist that it is a disorganized and formless collection of colour-patches, and cannot possibly be a picture of the west door of Chartres Cathedral. It may be necessary, and it may be possible, to point out to him the outline of the door of the cathedral. It may be possible to make him see something that he had not at first seen, in spite of the fact that he, like his instructor, has for twenty minutes had his eyes open and turned in the right direction in a good light. And what he is brought to see is not an 'aesthetic' property, but a straightforward visual, visible feature of the object before him, which has been *revealed* to him, though not by removing any veil.

Two pages of Greek that look very much the same to a child *look* very different to a classical scholar. It is not just that he understands their meaning and the child does not. It would be far more difficult for the child than for the scholar to remember which is which or to make a copy of one of them. It has been said that 'expertise is 90% memory'; it would be fairer to say that memory is 90% expertise.

The non-deductive and non-inductive modes of apprehension that are illustrated by these examples have a depth and range of importance which could hardly be exaggerated, but which has seldom, in the writings of philosophers, been anything but minimized or ignored. The examples I have already considered are sufficient to establish that there are such modes of reasoning and apprehension, but they give no sufficient indication of their range and power. What is most easily overlooked is the role that these modes play within the logical and scientific disciplines from which positivists draw their restrictive paradigms. As we have seen, a man might have Galileo's power to predict the behaviour of balls rolling down inclined planes and might still lack Galileo's understanding of the functional relationships exemplified by that behaviour. This further dimension of understanding involves the perception of patterns and analogies whose discovery and description take us off the narrow beaten tracks of induction and deduction. To devise and to support a physical theory that will explain the phenomena and provide a basis for the predictions is to go far beyond the observation and prediction to which too many philosophers of science have sought to reduce the processes of scientific discovery and proof. Prediction and observation are crucially important in science, but the contribution of a scientific theory to our knowledge and understanding is not always directly proportional to its predictive power. We cannot understand or describe the controversy between the Ptolemaic and Copernican accounts of the relation between the earth and the sun if we confine our attention to the observations and predictions that are admittedly crucial in settling the dispute, and ignore the extent to which the controversy involves the perception in and application to the phenomena of patterns, pictures, models. The connection of this case with my more informal examples is shown by Professor N. R. Hanson when, in a book felicitously entitled *Patterns of Discovery*, he raises the question whether Kepler and Tycho Brahe see the same thing when they look east at dawn.

Logic, too, involves the perception and revelation of patterns in complex mazes of particularity. Aristotle recognizes and describes a structure in syllogistic argument which might well be missed by somebody who nevertheless had Aristotle's power to say of any syllogistic argument that it was valid or invalid, and why it was valid or invalid. Aristotle's formal theory of the syllogism is so far from being necessary for the recognition that this or that syllogistic argument is valid that, on the contrary, he could not propound a correct theory unless he already knew of every particular syllogistic argument whether it was valid or invalid.

This example shows how close is the connection between the role of informal apprehension of patterns and the epistemological primacy of particular cases. Both points are more clearly visible if we consider some growing branch of logic, such as deontic logic. Aristotelian syllogistic is so familiar and so well established that we can easily overlook the character of the procedures by which it came to be established. But if Professor A. N. Prior were to show that in Professor G. H. von Wright's system of deontic logic it is possible to derive as a theorem that whatever is not forbidden is obligatory (e.g. that it follows from the fact that wearing a green tie in Hall is not forbidden that wearing a green tie is compulsory) neither Prior nor von Wright would think of von Wright as having revealed a surprising and hitherto overlooked feature of the notions of obligation and permission: they would both recognize that Prior's example was a *counter-example* to von Wright's theory, one that showed that the cases with which his theory was concerned do not exhibit the pattern that was attributed to them by the theory.

We come close to the bearing of these considerations on the nature of theology and religion when we see how centrally important they are for literature and morality. Henry James's novel, *The Ambassadors*, is the story of a moral discovery, of a growth in Strether's knowledge and self-knowledge. Strether came to Paris to rescue Chad from what Mrs Newsome, and Strether himself at first, had seen as a dangerous entanglement, a *liaison dangereuse*. In pursuing this aim Strether learns more about Chad, about himself, about Paris, about Europe and America, about life and love and the world in general, than he had known before. His eyes are opened wider and turned in new directions. It is not just that he learns some particular facts and circumstances that were unknown to him before, though that is an important part of his progress from ignorance to knowledge. He also sees patterns and connections in and between facts and circumstances that were in one good sense already well known to him. He understands better than he understood before items and fragments of information that were already available to him before he left the United States and Mrs Newsome.

T. S. Eliot has in mind the same kind of growth and discovery
when he speaks of coming to 'a new and shocking valuation of
all that we have been and seen'. One may by taking stock come
to such a new and shocking valuation without adding any new
items to the pattern, without even noticing any hitherto unnoticed
item, but just by recognizing for the first time the nature and
structure of the pattern that is to be seen in the items.

In *The Ambassadors* James underlines his presentation of
Strether's progress as a journey from ignorance to knowledge,
from incomprehension to a deeper understanding, by what has
every appearance of being a conscious and deliberate emphasis
on the epistemic verbs with which the narration is thickly
encrusted: Strether is repeatedly represented as knowing,
understanding, perceiving, seeing, recognizing, learning, realizing. And all these words here carry their customary commitments to the *truth* of what is known, understood, recognized
and perceived. When James reports that Strether saw something to be so, or now recognized something to be the case,
he commits his narration, if not himself, to holding that it
was so.

These examples, like those used by Wisdom, are designed to
show limitations both in the positivistic conception of fact and in
the positivistic conception of logic. When Strether by reflection
on facts already known to him reaches a new conclusion about
the situation of himself or Chad, he comes to know answers
to factual questions to which he did not at first know the
answers. This shows that new observational or experimental
data are not always required for the settlement of a factual
question. And the reflection by which he reaches his new
conclusions, though *a priori*, armchair reflection, is not deductive. This shows that reflection on the relations of ideas need
not conform to the mathematical models of Hume and Ayer.
These are the points made by Wisdom's favourite examples of
the accountant and the lawyer, and by numerous analogous
examples that are well described by Mr R. W. Newell in
The Concept of Philosophy.

When Wisdom in his paper on 'Gods' remarks that the existence
of God is neither an experimental issue nor one to be settled by
calculation, he is not therefore to be understood as denying
that it is a factual issue and one to be dealt with by rational

investigation and reflection. In his famous and much misunderstood analogy of the gardener (*Philosophy and Psycho-analysis*, pp. 154–5), and in his comments on it, he shows that an issue may be an issue about what is so, and may call for sustained rational inquiry, even when the text-book patterns of inductive and deductive reasoning are unnecessary and insufficient for the conduct of that inquiry.

The analogy of the dispute about the existence or non-existence of an invisible gardener would be valuable even if its purpose and effect were no more than to produce a counter-example to positivistic restrictions on the range of intelligible discussion and dispute. But the analogy has a more direct and detailed bearing on questions about the nature of the conflict between an atheist and a religious believer. It shows that the theist and the atheist may be disagreeing about a matter of fact, about what in fact the nature of the world is, even when there are no primary data available to the one that are not available to the other, and when neither of them has any expectation as to the future that the other does not have. It shows that a dispute about the character of the world may persist when there are no particular, concrete, detailed features of the world that are seen by one party to the dispute but are hidden from the other; just as there may be a dispute about the character of a picture, a novel or a human being, even when each party to the dispute has before his eyes all the items and incidents that are before the eyes of the other.

One might describe such a dispute by saying that it concerns the *internal* character and relations of the thing or person, event or situation, whose character is in dispute. The disputants cannot resort to any crucial observation or experiment, any procedure of withdrawing a veil or turning a stone, that will reveal to either of them a hitherto hidden object or feature about whose presence or absence they have been in conflict. This shows that their dispute is necessarily not a standard inductive or predictive dispute; for it is the leading feature of such a dispute that it should involve disagreement on what would actually occur or would be disclosed if certain practical steps were taken which could in principle even if they cannot in practice be taken. If the dispute were an ordinary dispute about an ordinary gardener, it would in principle be settleable by taking steps of a kind that, in Wisdom's case, have, *ex hypothesi*, already been taken without leading to a settlement of the dispute.

It is clear even from this brief exposition how great an advance Wisdom's account represents over the positivistic account that it was designed to supersede. It shows that disputes about the existence of gods are neither deductive nor inductive nor unintelligible. It does the theist and the atheist the honour of recognizing that they are engaged in a genuine conflict, that, in Wisdom's own phrase, the dispute between them, and the remarks that each of them makes in support of his answer to the question concerning which they are in dispute, 'have a logic'. And Wisdom rightly represents these disputes and these remarks as having a logic without wrongly representing them as having a deductive (reductive) logic or an inductive logic. Wisdom's account has a value and importance of which this brief sketch gives only the barest indication. I believe that it comes nearer than any account offered before or since to giving an accurate characterization of the nature of disputes about the existence of God.

This account nevertheless leaves me with a feeling of dissatisfaction which I will now try to articulate in the hope of throwing a little more light on what Wisdom has illuminated. My dissatisfaction is akin to that of some of the orthodox theologians who have best understood what Wisdom is saying about their arguments and doctrines. (It is significant that Wisdom's treatment, which is offered as a neutral account of the logic of theological disputes, has found more favour among atheists and agnostics than among their theological opponents, and that some of the Christian believers who have been most favourably impressed with Wisdom's treatment have also been among those who have least well understood it.)

One very general way of giving expression to my reservations about Wisdom's account would be to ask whether the early Church would recognize what is left to it by Wisdom as an interpretation of its central doctrines. He leaves those doctrines much nearer to the shepherds and to mother's knee than the crude reductive account, but he still leaves them further away than most orthodox theologians would be prepared to allow. Though he represents theological claims as deserving to be called claims of fact, as being recognizably *assertions*, so that there is according to him scope for the application within theology of the concepts of truth and falsehood, and scope for the employment of argument and reasoning, the question remains whether he leaves sufficient scope, or scope of the right kind.

While Wisdom gives us an interpretation of the sentence 'God exists' according to which it makes an assertion that is either true or false, it seems to me doubtful whether his interpretation preserves the assertion as the *kind* of assertion that it is – namely, an assertion of the *existence* of a *substance*, and, what is more, of a *personal* substance. He shows that the words have an intelligible use in which they do not express the conclusion either of a purely *a priori* or of an inductive investigation, but it seems to me that he does not and could not show that that intelligible use is the use to which that form of words has traditionally been put and is still put by orthodox Christian believers. As Wisdom himself indicates, it is possible to *re*-interpret assertions of the existence or non-existence of ancient Greek gods on the lines on which he interprets assertions of the existence or non-existence of God. But Wisdom's purpose was not to *re*-interpret but to *interpret*, and it is a suspicion that he has, though to a much lesser extent that some of his predecessors, reinterpreted statements about God's existence, that leads me to conclude that he has partly failed in his object. He has *de-transcendentalized* statements about God's existence, and the question arises whether theology can continue to be what it has traditionally been if the transcendentalist element is removed from it or is drastically reduced.

Wisdom is certainly careful not to over-emphasize, though he does sufficiently allow for, the element of attitude, response, feeling, 'picture-preference', that rightly belongs to theological affirmations and denials. He can place this element in its proper perspective because he shows that between atheists and theists there is genuine conflict about how things are, that there is more to theological dispute than a choice of notations or modes of projection. My question is whether the 'more' is what it must be if we are to be left with theology rather than with a misleading rational reconstruction of theology. Though the difficulties arise here in a much less acute form than they do with some cruder accounts, I think that the same difficulties do arise. Is Wisdom's version of Christian theism in its turn incapable of preserving the facilities for exclusiveness and for heresy that are more evidently destroyed by some more explicitly reductive theories? Does he too make of Christian theology one among many possible sets of terms for conducting a kind of reflection that need not be conducted in *theological* categories at all?

These are not rhetorical questions expecting the answer 'Yes'. No straightforward answers can be given to them at least until we have looked again and independently at the concept of transcendence and its role in theological thought. This is the central problem not only of this course but also of contemporary philosophy of religion in general, and I shall be returning to it in a later lecture. At this stage I will only state the problem as clearly and starkly as possible, and this can best be done by giving an outline of how the notion of transcendence can be shown to be unnecessary in all the non-theological fields in which it has been invoked, and then asking whether theology is different in sufficiently relevant respects to require the preservation of this notion for its purposes alone.

The recent advances in general epistemology to which Wisdom himself has most signally contributed have shown us that hypotheses about the existence of transcendent substances are neither a necessary nor a possible expedient for the purposes for which they have traditionally been adopted: that ontological theories are the effects of epistemological misunderstandings combined with epistemological insights, and that the insights can be preserved when the misunderstandings have been exposed and the theories have been given up.

Behind all the varieties of philosophical idiom there lies a common preoccupation with epistemological problems, with questions about meaning, truth, knowledge and justification. These epistemic concepts are both so basic and so pervasive that a recurrent pattern can be perceived through the important logical differences between one kind of inquiry and another and the corresponding differences between the epistemological disputes about the different kinds of inquiry. I can therefore illustrate the pattern by one main example without serious risk of misrepresenting its other applications, of which in any case I have already said something in my first lecture. The problem of other minds is a specially apt example, both because it is one that has particularly and profitably interested Wisdom, and because of the direct relevance of questions about the existence of human minds to questions about the existence of divine minds.

Our ultimate evidence for propositions about the minds of others consists of propositions about their bodily behaviour. Like every other trans-type inference from propositions of one kind to propositions of another kind, the logical relation between propositions about other minds and their ultimate grounds has been misrepresented in three main ways, which all derive from the same underlying misconception, the idea that all logical relations are either inductive or deductive. The sceptic about other minds recognizes that the relation in this case is neither inductive nor deductive, and therefore concludes that the behavioural evidence gives no support to the psychological conclusion. The behaviourist tries to save our knowledge of other minds by representing the evidence as deductively related to the conclusion, the statement about another mind as equivalent to the behavioural evidence on which it rests. The dualist takes the other horn of the misconceived dilemma: he sees both that we do know about other minds and that our conclusions about other minds are not identical with the evidence on which they rest; that a statement about a mind says something that is not said by a set of statements about a body, however comprehensive. He therefore misconstrues the psychological conclusion as being *inductively* supported by its evidence, since he is impressed by the fact that there is 'something more' in the conclusion than in the evidence, and by the fact that in this respect the trans-type inference is more closely analogous to an inductive than to a deductive inference. But the analogy is fatally incomplete. A conclusion can be inductively established only when a conclusion of the same type as itself has been established in the past without induction, and only when there are available even in the case of the present inductively established conclusion direct, non-inductive means of confirming it; and so no conclusion can be *ultimately* established by induction any more than by deduction.

Dualism is the form that transcendentalism takes in this dispute. Here as in the other comparable disputes the transcendentalist invokes the existence of a transcendent substance 'over and above' the 'manifestations' which are construed as indirect indications of the presence of something distinct from and independent of themselves. The sceptic draws attention to what he sees as a logical gap between the evidence and the conclusion. The transcendentalist invokes his metaphysical substance to stop the gap. The reductionist, meanwhile, fearing that if there were allowed to be a gap it would be necessary to concur in the invocation of the substance, is prompted to *identify* the evidence with the conclusion for which it is evidence.

Though this identification of meaning with verification is explicitly made only by the reductionist or positivist, it is a mistake that underlies the mistakes of all three parties to this and to every analogous dispute. The evidence that something is or has a mind does not exhaust the meaning of the proposition that it is or has a mind. This easily gives rise to the illusion that there must be something – some (one) *thing* – which we can identify as the thing that closes the gap between the evidence and the conclusion. When the sceptic rejects the conclusion because the evidence is not logically sufficient for it he presupposes that we can have a justification for a conclusion only when the evidence *is* logically sufficient for it. The transcendentalist recognizes that what is ordinarily counted as the ultimate evidence does not entail the conclusion. Since he also recognizes that the conclusion is nevertheless justified he tries to supply something else – an insight, an intuition, a transcendental mode of argument – which, when added to what is ordinarily recognized to be the ultimate evidence, *will* entail the conclusion: so that he too, in spite of his fundamental opposition to the sceptic and to the reductionist on other and important points, shares their verificationist prejudice.

The position may be represented by an analogy with weighing on a pair of scales. The sceptic rightly observes that the weight in the evidence scale never balances the weight in the conclusion scale, and wrongly concludes that the conclusion is unjustified. The reductionist sees that the conclusion is justified, and wrongly concludes that the evidence does balance the weight of the conclusion. The transcendentalist recognizes both that the conclusion is justified and that the evidence does not balance its weight. He therefore offers a *makeweight* –

something that will secure a balance between what is in the evidence scale and what is in the conclusion scale. All three theorists, with varying degrees of explicitness, assume that the scales must be in logical balance before the conclusion can be said to be justified: they are all verificationists.

On the road back from these generalities to our specific problem about theological transcendence, it will be an advantage to consider a particular case of disputation about the presence or absence of a *finite* mind. Suppose that we were faced with a creature found on a distant planet or produced in a mathematical or biochemical laboratory, of which some asserted and others denied that it had a mind. How would the dispute be settled? If we are supplied with all the primary data that we need, about the reactions and responses of the disputed object or creature, we may find that in order to answer the question 'Does it have a mind?' all we need is an adequate grasp of the concept of mind, an understanding of what it is for something to have a mind. In such a situation we are tempted to put our question in the form 'What is the difference between a mere machine or a mere animal and a creature with a mind?' The very form of the question tempts us to forget all that we have laboriously learned about universals and family resemblances, to go back to the essentialism, the Platonist realism, the idea that the meaning of a word is an object, from which Wittgenstein strove to liberate us. Wittgenstein tried to teach us *differences*, but we are tempted to look for *the* difference. When we use the treacherous singular – 'What is *the* difference?' – we are betrayed into looking for *the* criterion by which we discriminate a creature with a mind from a mere machine, for *the* mental *element* that is present in a creature that has a mind and absent from a creature that has not. If we follow Wittgenstein's admittedly dangerous advice to *look* rather than *think*, if we describe to ourselves numerous actual and possible cases of minds, of machines, of things on the border-lines between minds and machines, mere animals and persons, we see that there is no single element common to all minds, and help to save ourselves from generating a transcendent psychic substance to fulfil the role of what distinguishes a creature that has a mind from a thing that has none. And an important part of the procedure that saves us from this transcendentalism

about minds is the setting out for ourselves of the complete continuity between cases that are undoubtedly cases of minds and
cases that are undoubtedly not cases of minds.

If a creature or object is in all external respects indistinguishable from one that has a mind, then it is one that has a mind.
And to say this is not to say that the conclusion that it has a
mind is a restatement of the evidence that shows that it has a
mind.

Are divine minds different? Is the relation between propositions about superhuman minds and the ultimate evidence for
those propositions so different from the relation between
propositions about human minds and the ultimate evidence for
them that a transcendentalist mode of inference or the hypothesis of a transcendent mental substance, which is unnecessary
and impossible in the one case, should be possible and necessary
in the other?

In all the standard traditional metaphysical disputes –
about mind, matter, time, necessity, value – it now appears
that transcendentalist ontology results from epistemological
confusion. Is theology so special, so different, that there can be
a transcendentalist theological ontology which is not the result
of epistemological confusion? It looks at this stage as if we must
find scope for transcendentalist ontology if we are to preserve
traditional theology. It also looks as if all the weight of recent
metaphysical philosophy is against any hope of preserving a
transcendentalist ontology in theology or anywhere else. It
looks in consequence as if the evidence of recent metaphysical
philosophy counts strongly against any hope of preserving
traditional theology in its traditional form.

I have been critical of Wisdom's account of the logic of God.
I have voiced the suspicion that he has not fully achieved the
neutrality on doctrinal issues that he implicitly claims for his
treatment. But his writings constitute the most valuable single
characterization of the logic of theological reasoning. His
work has the great merit of concentrating our attention on the
connections and parallels that are ignored by philosophers in
search of neat distinctions and tidy criteria. He attends to the
variety and multiplicity of theological utterances, and to
the overlapping and criss-crossing between theology and other
forms of reasoning; not only between theology and science or

logic, but also between theology and morals, criticism and law. He also places a welcome and unfashionable emphasis on the *objectivity* of theological inquiry. He resists both the positivistic rejection of theology for its failure to conform to the shape of logic or science, and also the irrationalism of some defenders of theology who have themselves accepted the positivistic principle that all forms of reasoning must be either quasi-mathematical or quasi-scientific, and who have therefore ceased to hold that theological reasoning is reasoning. In his rejection of scepticism, reductionism and transcendentalism about theology he applies to it methods and principles which have shed light on many other inquiries and branches of knowledge. His case against theological scepticism and theological reductionism is luminous and convincing. We shall need to consider again whether he does not leave theological transcendence under a cloud that must be dispersed if theology is to be seen to stand where once it stood.

5 · Stories

In the last two lectures I have considered some accounts of
theological inquiry which attempt to preserve the *factual*
character of theology, its claim to be saying something about
what is so in the world we live in, but which nevertheless give
due weight to the difficulties that have been urged against many
primitive and traditional interpretations of some characteristically theological affirmations. My reflections on these accounts
have led me to a problem rather than to a solution; to a problem
which may be expressed in a number of questions about the
impact of recent philosophy on the assessment of the nature
and value of theological thought. Can theology survive the
anti-transcendentalist results of twentieth-century philosophy?
Has theology over-invested in types of philosophy that are a
poor market today? Does it now live under a threat of philosophical bankruptcy, and, if so, is there any possible policy of
prudent reinvestment which may be able to restore its fortunes?

The importance of this problem, and the impossibility of
escaping it, will be underlined if we now go on to explore an
alternative route which I have mentioned but have not yet
examined. While some defenders of theology have been engaged in reinterpreting doctrines which in their traditional
forms are widely agreed to be false, others have taken the much
more radical step of jettisoning all factual assertions, all dogmas
or doctrines about *what is so*. This sounds, at first hearing,
less like a defence of theology than an unconditional surrender
to its enemies. It sounds more like a complete rejection of
religion than a reinterpretation of it. But the thinkers I now
wish to consider do not think of themselves as atheists, or as
non-Christians. They would regard themselves as preservers of
what is *essential* to religion, of what is left when *mere doctrine*
has been removed.

One who belongs to this school of thought says in effect,
'I am a Christian, *but*: I do not believe in the Incarnation, or

F

in the doctrine of the Trinity, or in the Resurrection of Jesus Christ; I do not affirm the Apostles' Creed, or the Nicene Creed, or the Athanasian Creed; I do not believe that Christ is the Son of God, or that God made heaven and earth and all things visible and invisible'.

My comments on this approach will be made with special reference to two of its most notable representatives: Matthew Arnold, whose *Literature and Dogma* was a pioneering contribution to this movement; and Professor R. B. Braithwaite, whose Eddington Lecture, *An Empiricist's View of the Nature of Religious Belief*, is the most philosophically sophisticated of numerous recent writings in the same vein.

Although the explicit abandonment of the traditional claim of theology to make assertions about the world and its nature raises issues which need separate and special treatment, it will be clear that the comments that I have already made on a number of less radical accounts are applicable, *a fortiori*, to the accounts offered by Arnold and Braithwaite. I have argued that theology must involve the making of assertions which depend on evidence that is publicly available in the ordinary world we live in, but which say more than that such public evidence is available, and which are capable of being objectively known to be true or false. The account that I called 'reductionism' wrongly identifies theological assertions with the non-theological assertions that are offered as grounds for them. Fideism, and all accounts that make religious belief exclusively a matter of will or choice, and the sceptical form of agnosticism which maintains that it is in principle impossible to determine whether religious assertions are true or false, preserve the right kind of assertions but destroy their indispensable objectivity. For reasons that I have already largely given, I therefore reject the conclusions of Arnold and Braithwaite. They, too, put old forms to unacceptable new uses.

But Arnold and Braithwaite deserve fuller and more particular consideration. Their detailed arguments must be examined and answered. What is more important is that here, as so often in philosophy, we shall find that mistaken doctrines are not *merely* mistaken. In stating and defending their false conclusions about the nature of Christian theology, these writers reveal for us, even if in a form distorted and heightened by caricature, aspects of theology and religion which may be obscured by other accounts that are in other respects more balanced and more accurate. Their views are prompted by, and therefore valuably underline, elements in the present situation of theology that are intrinsically important, and which can serve to clarify for us some features of theology in general. They have made false moves, but they have made moves which would not have been tempting if it were not for the presence in theology of some characteristics which other accounts have insufficiently stressed. If General de Gaulle had a tiny snub nose he would never be represented in political cartoons as having an elephant's trunk.

Arnold begins by declaring that *morality* is what is essential to religion, and in particular to the Christian religion. Righteousness is the head and corner-stone of the theology of the Old Testament, and in the New Testament charity is raised above faith and hope. But it is clear that morality is not *identical* with religion. What must be added to morality to make it into religion? Arnold answers that the missing ingredient is *emotion*. Religion is 'morality touched by emotion':

And if someone now asks: But what *is* this application of emotion to morality, and by what marks may we know it? – we can quite easily satisfy him; not, indeed, by any disquisition of our own, but in a much better way, by examples. 'By the dispensation of Providence to mankind,' says Quintilian, 'goodness gives men most satisfaction.' That is morality. 'The path of the just is as the shining light which shineth more and more unto the perfect day.' That is morality touched with emotion, or religion. 'Hold off from sensuality,' says Cicero; 'for, if you have given yourself up to it, you will find yourself unable to think of anything else.' That is morality. 'Blessed are the pure in heart,' says Jesus Christ; 'for they shall see God.' That is religion. 'We all want to live honestly, but cannot,' says the Greek maxim-maker. That is morality. 'O wretched man that I am, who shall deliver me from the body of this death!' says St Paul. That is religion. 'Would thou wert of as good conversation in deed as in word!' is morality. 'Not every one that saith unto me, Lord, Lord, shall enter into the Kingdom of Heaven, but he that doeth the will of my Father which is in heaven,' is religion. 'Live as you were meant to live!' is morality. 'Lay hold on eternal life!' is religion.

Or we may take the contrast within the bounds of the Bible itself. 'Love not sleep, lest thou come to poverty,' is morality. But: 'My meat is to do the will of him that sent me, and to finish his work', is religion. Or we may even observe a third stage between these two stages, which shows to us the transition from one to the other. 'If thou givest thy soul the desires that please her, she will make thee a laughing stock to thine enemies,' – that is morality. 'He that resisteth pleasure crowneth his life' – that is morality with the tone heightened, passing, or trying to pass, into religion. 'Flesh and blood cannot inherit the kingdom of God,' – there the passage is made, and we have religion. Our religious examples are here all taken from the Bible, and from the Bible such examples can best be taken; but we might also find them elsewhere. 'Oh that my lot might lead me in the path of holy innocence of thought and deed, the path which august laws ordain, laws which in the highest heaven had their birth, neither did the race of mortal man beget them, nor shall oblivion ever put them to sleep; the power of God is mighty in them, and groweth not old!' That is from Sophocles, but it is as much religion as any of the things which we have quoted as religious. Like them, it is not the mere enjoining of conduct, but it is this enjoining touched, strengthened, and almost transformed, by the addition of feeling.

Chapter I, § 2.

It is just because Arnold is so right in his classification of his examples of morality and religion that we can see clearly how fundamentally wrong he is about the relation between morality and religion. What he identifies as examples of religious affirmations *are* religious affirmations, and they do differ markedly from the examples of moral exhortation that he sets beside them. But the religious affirmations differ from the moral ones not only or mainly by the addition of emotion, but by the addition of *doctrine*. Some of them refer explicitly to God and his Kingdom, to Jesus Christ as the Son of God the Father, or to eternal life. Others derive their religious character from the context of doctrine in which they are embodied, and would cease to be religious, however moral and emotional they remained, if they were removed from that context.

Arnold explicitly rejects all such doctrines. Like the 'masses' whom he wishes to recall to a sense of the 'natural truth' of Christianity as a moral message, he rejects all miracles, all theological doctrines that relate to the supernatural or the transcendental. He bitterly mocks the Incarnation and the doctrine of the Trinity. In a parody that became so notorious that Arnold omitted it from the popular edition of *Literature and Dogma*, he pilloried God the Father as 'a sort of infinitely magnified and improved Lord Shaftesbury' whose dealings with his people are conducted by two other Lord Shaftesburys. The Apostles' Creed is 'popular science'; the Nicene Creed is 'learned science'; the Athanasian Creed is 'learned science with a strong dash of temper'. All such 'fairy tales' and 'abstract ideas' are irrelevant to true religion. And they are worse than irrelevant, because as long as religion is associated with such nonsense, not only intelligent people but even the masses will reject the religion as well as the nonsense. The Bible must not be 'made to depend on a story, or set of asserted facts, which it is impossible to verify; and which hard-headed people, therefore, treat as either an imposture, or a fairy tale that discredits all which is found in connection with it'.

The unverifiablity of the doctrines of the Churches is a recurrent theme in Arnold's polemic. Everything which is not *sure*, not *verified*, must be given up. And the most dangerous idea of all, that of 'a great Personal First Cause, who thinks and loves, the moral and intelligent Governor of the Universe', must be set at the heart of the bonfire. For if this idea is once accepted, the other fairy tales can be smuggled in with some show of reason and common sense. Those who can be induced to swallow the elephant will not strain at the camel and the gnat. The whole system of unverified and unverifiable abstract ideas must be repudiated; it is useless to tinker with the parts.

This first, destructive phase of Arnold's argument is indistinguishable in tone and content from many an atheistical pamphlet. But when the 'house of cards' has toppled, and just when it seems clear that the site is to be bequeathed to the Rationalist Press Association, Arnold lays foundations for the rebuilding of the Christian religion on the vacant lot. In the spirit of his sub-title, 'An Essay Towards a Better Apprehension of the Bible', he maintains that the religion of the Bible, far from deserving the fate to which he has consigned the theology of the Churches, can be seen in its true light and at its inestimable value only when the metaphysical and transcendental undergrowth of theology has been scorched and scattered. Just as the Greeks endure as an unparalleled but not inimitable pattern of achievement in the fine arts, so must the Hebrews be kept before us as never-failing witnesses to the deliverances of the sense of conduct, 'the sense which has to do with three-fourths of human life'. For two thousand years their light has been darkened by the glass of theological fashion and their lineaments have been distorted by the mould of metaphysical form:

> Anyone does a good deed who removes stumbling-blocks out of the way of our feeling and profiting by the witness left by this people. And so, instead of making our Hebrew speakers mean, in their use of the word God, a scientific affirmation which never entered into their heads, and about which many will dispute, let us content ourselves with making them mean, as a matter of scientific fact and experience, what they really did mean as such, and what is unchallengable. Let us put into their 'Eternal' and 'God' no more science than they did: – *the enduring power, not ourselves which makes for righteousness.* They meant more by these names, but they meant this; and this they grasped fully. And the sense which this will give us for their words is at least solid; so that we may find it of use as a guide to steady us, and to give us a constant clue in following what they say.
>
> Chapter I, § 5

Arnold proceeds systematically to retranslate, to *mistranslate*, the Old Testament, *passim*, in order to expunge all traces of the doctrine of a personal God. Whenever a prophet or psalmist speaks of 'the Lord', Arnold reads 'The Eternal': '*The Eternal* is my shepherd.' And he claims that this is what the words of the Old Testament *really* mean. The God of Israel is not a personal agent at work in the universe, but a vague impersonal power outside ourselves that reinforces our efforts to live good lives. We must reserve the name of God for the power that reinforces our moral aspirations. We shall then be giving the name to 'a certain admitted reality' instead of to an uncertain and unverifiable person. We may retain the doctrine of the immortality of the soul, but only if we understand it as a figurative reminder of the sense of life that accompanies virtuous action. We must scorn the foolish theologians and their talk of the wisdom and the goodness *of* God: wisdom and goodness *are* God. The false doctrine that God is Love must be stood on its head as the true doctrine that Love is God.

The *vagueness* is not only admitted, but emphasized. The danger of the personal God of the Churches is that the idea of such a God is clear, and the masses are able to see that it is clearly false. Arnold's own conception of God has the advantage of being so vague that its opponents are not provided with such facilities for suggesting that it is false or unverifiable.

This is the crucial advantage that Arnold claims for his account. By its vagueness it escapes and circumvents 'the difficulties which torment theology'. He does indeed circumvent those difficulties; but at what price? He dispenses with what is indispensable to Christian theology. His unavowed conclusion is that the Christian religion is false, but that Christian morality is worthy to be saved from the flames to which the dogmas and doctrines and abstract ideas of Christian theology must be committed. Honesty and clarity require him to say that because the Christian religion is unverified and unverifiable, he *rejects* it. What he does say is that what is usually thought to be meant by the propositions of the Christian religion is unverified and unverifiable, and that therefore those propositions must mean something else that he *can* believe. This is a gross *non sequitur*, but it is not a rare aberration, not an idiosyncratic lapse on the part of Arnold. It is a common response to the predicament that Arnold found himself in.

Arnold was drawn by his education in two radically opposed directions. His Christian upbringing had left an indelible mark on his mind and character. But he was also familiar with and sympathetic to movements in the scientific and philosophical thought of the nineteenth and earlier centuries which persuaded him that the doctrinal content of the Christian religion as it had been taught to him was philosophically and scientifically unacceptable. He therefore sought for, and deceived himself into thinking that he had found, a way of interpreting the traditional formulae of the Christian religion according to which their content would be compatible with his scientific and philosophical beliefs: something that could be called Christianity and that he could still with a good conscience affirm and defend. Poseidon is dead. Long live Poseidon.

Professor Braithwaite's account is closely akin to Arnold's, both in its content and in its motives and sources. He quotes Arnold, whom he describes as 'a great but neglected Christian thinker'. But he differs sufficiently from Arnold to need separate discussion, and the main difference, from which some of the other differences arise, is that Braithwaite expresses himself in an idiom that owes much to philosophical developments that took place after Arnold's death. He makes use of the concepts and procedures of twentieth-century analytical and linguistic philosophy, and his account is a near neighbour of the logical positivist doctrine that traditional theology is literally senseless.

Like the positivists, Braithwaite holds that nothing can be a branch of objective knowledge unless it is either *a priori* and analytical or scientific and empirical, and he agrees with them that theology does not meet either of these requirements. He must therefore look elsewhere for the meaning of theological propositions if he is not to be forced to the positivist conclusion that they have no meaning. He finds the essence of religion exactly where Arnold found it, in morality.

But Braithwaite, like Arnold, has to recognize that morality is not identical with religion, and that he too is called upon to explain how morality differs from religion. He first points to two differences which he regards as being of minor importance: (1) Religion is more concerned with the *inner* life of man, than morality, as he understands it, is or needs to be. Morality is concerned with acts and their consequences; religion is concerned also with men's motives and characters. (2) Religion involves ritual and ceremony, neither of which is involved in morality. But Braithwaite recognizes that these two additions are insufficient to convert morality into religion, and in particular that nothing can count as a religion unless it makes important use of assertions of propositions capable of being true or false. He therefore suggests that the essential difference between religion and morality consists in the fact that, in its religious forms, morality is associated with certain 'stories':

> The really important difference, I think, is to be found in the fact that the intentions to pursue the behaviour policies, which may be the same for different religions, are associated with thinking of different *stories* (or sets of stories). By a story I shall here mean a proposition or set of propositions which are straightforwardly empirical propositions capable of empirical test and which are thought of by the religious man in connexion with his resolution to follow the way of life advocated by his religion. On the assumption that the ways of life advocated by Christianity and by Buddhism are essentially the same, it will be the fact that the intention to follow this way of life is associated in the mind of a Christian with thinking of one set of stories (the Christian stories) while it is associated in the mind of a Buddhist with thinking of another set of stories (the Buddhist stories) which enables a Christian assertion to be distinguished from a Buddhist one. A religious assertion will, therefore, have a propositional element which is lacking in a purely moral assertion, in that it will refer to a story as well as to an intention. The reference to the story is not an assertion of the story taken as a matter of empirical fact: it is a telling of the story, or an alluding to the story, in the way in which one can tell, or allude to, the story of a novel with which one is acquainted. To assert the whole set of assertions of the Christian religion is both to tell the Christian doctrinal story and to confess allegiance to the Christian way of life.   (pp. 23–4)

Braithwaite goes on to explain, with even greater candour than Arnold, that his account has the advantage of saving theology from much embarrassment. Conventional theologians are distracted and misguided by a feeling that their theological assertions must be *true*. But for religious purposes, as Braithwaite conceives them, the truth or falsehood of the stories of the Christian religion is unimportant. It is not even essential, according to him, that the set of Christian stories should be mutually consistent. The only relevant test is whether the stories are effective in reinforcing the Christian resolution to follow an 'agapeistic' way of life. In one place he suggests that there may be a positive advantage to a religion in having mutually inconsistent stories included in the set of stories associated with its moral policies: that 'a story may provide better support for a long range policy of action if it contains inconsistencies':

> The Christian set of stories, for example, contains both a pantheistic sub-set of stories in which everything is a part of God and a dualistic Manichaean sub-set of stories well represented by St Ignatius Loyola's allegory of a conflict between the forces of righteousness under the banner of Christ and the forces of darkness under Lucifer's banner. And the Marxist religion's set of stories contains both stories about an inevitable perfect society and stories about a class war. In the case of both religions the first sub-set of stories provide confidence, the second spurs to action.   (p. 30)

Braithwaite tells us that he chose the word 'story' as being a neutral term, less likely to cause offence than Arnold's contemptuous rhetoric against 'fairy tales' and 'abstract ideas'. But the orthodox may be forgiven if they find the word 'story' as pejorative as some of Arnold's epithets, and if they are provoked rather than pacified when they find Braithwaite speaking on pages 30–31 of 'one story common to all the moral theistic religions, which has proved of great psychological value in enabling men to persevere in carrying out their religious behaviour-policies – the story that in so doing they are doing the will of God'.

This last sentence brings into high relief the contrast between Christian orthodoxy and the interpretation given by Braithwaite to its doctrinal formulae. The orthodox believer offers the *fact* that what he is doing is in accordance with the will of God as a *reason* for doing it. Braithwaite sees the relation between religious stories or doctrines and moral conduct and moral resolution not as a logical but as a *causal* relation. A religious story is to be prescribed and administered and swallowed as if it were a drug. Its function is to stimulate. It is by telling themselves stories that religious men are reinforced in their determination to live a particular kind of life.

At this point Braithwaite has parted company with Arnold, who wholly rejects Christian stories and doctrines as false or unverifiable and does not countenance their use even as stimulants to resolution. Braithwaite is rightly too sensitive to the need for a 'propositional element in religion' to abjure altogether the traditional formulae of the Christian faith. He pours new wine into the old bottles that Arnold would cheerfully consign to the dustbin. But there are other respects in which Arnold, for all his iconoclasm, is closer than Braithwaite to traditional orthodoxy. His polemic against conventional religion is based on a passionate desire for the truth and consistency that Braithwaite is prepared to sacrifice for psychological efficacy. Another and related difference is that Braithwaite is a subjectivist about the morality that he declares to be the essence of religion. His 'behaviour policies' are freely chosen, arbitrarily adopted, not recognized as having any independent and objective validity. Arnold's 'Eternal, not ourselves' is an objectively existing power, and it reinforces our attempts to pursue a righteousness that is also objective and independent of human will and choice. He offers an objective moral truth in place of a dogmatic theology that is objectively false. His religion is a response to something real and external, and not, like Braithwaite's, a spontaneous and ultimately ungrounded declaration of intention and resolve.

Arnold urges that 'literary experience, not reasoning' is the arbiter in matters of morals and religion. *Literature and Dogma* is a defence of literature against dogma. Religion is a province of the republic of letters. Braithwaite here again plays the same theme, but again with a characteristic variation. His 'stories' are the Bible designed to be read as literature, and literature designed to be read as the Bible. The novels of Dostoevsky, as well as the stories of the Old and New Testaments and *Pilgrim's Progress*, may serve the religious man's purpose of strengthening his moral resolves. But Arnold's high seriousness about literature is backed by his objectivism, his recognition that literature is a source and a repository of a moral knowledge and understanding that is found and not fashioned. Braithwaite's subjective metaphysic of morals leads him to demean literature to the status of an instrument for expressing or reinforcing moral intentions that have their origin in an antecedently adopted attitude. In the spirit of his positivistic inheritance, and against the grain of his own evidently deep feeling for literature, he treats it as if it were all and only 'fiction' in a somewhat pejorative sense of that word.

Christianity, even in the fatally maimed embodiment of it that is left to us by Arnold, retains a deep sense that the better conduct of life calls for a growth of knowledge, insight and understanding; for a struggle to pass from seeing as in a glass, darkly, to a clear light in which we may hope to know even as also we are known.

Braithwaite gives up so much of what belongs to Christianity that he, like Arnold, ought to say, 'I do not and cannot accept *Christianity*, but I offer you what remains when its essential falsehood has been exposed and excised.' He gives up even more than Arnold, in spite of his willingness to preserve at least the shells of the dogmatic theology that Arnold wholly abandons. For while they both truncate theology by reducing it to morality, the morality to which Braithwaite reduces it is itself truncated. Braithwaite allies himself so closely with Hare and Nowell-Smith, the Oxford apostles of a morality of action and choice, that he does not do justice even to a dimension of morality that he himself describes as a characteristically religious preoccupation – the dimension of the inner life, of motive and character. It is significant that he speaks of the inner life as inner *behaviour*: like the Oxford apostles he stresses action, choice, intention – the volitional and the conative – to the exclusion of motive, character, and all else in the wider range of morality that falls under the contemplative understanding rather than the will.

These last remarks must be allowed for the moment to remain abrupt and dogmatic: they will be elaborated and defended when I come to speak of philosophy of life. My present concern is with the epistemology of theological propositions, and with the question of whether the accounts of Arnold and Braithwaite, which I have criticized as caricatures of 'the propositional element in religion' may nevertheless have something positive to contribute to the direct description of the logical character of theology.

Their main positive contribution can best be seen by considering another point on which, for all their differences in other respects, they are closely agreed. In spite of their doctrinal heterodoxy, they are traditionalist and even conventionally evangelical in their emphasis on the *practical* nature of religion, and on the need for strenuous exertion after righteousness and charity. If Arnold's faith were Christianity, it would be of the most stringently muscular kind. In the manner of an evangelical preacher, he is perpetually insisting that religion *works*, and importunately calling upon the doubter to 'give it a trial'. Both the promise and the plea are those of the seller of patent medicines, worth a guinea a box, and may remind us again of Braithwaite's use of Christian stories as energizing drugs – the benzedrine of the people – strengthening the moral efforts of the consumer.

Some stress on results must be found in any faithful portrait of the Christian religion, which sets charity above faith and hope, and knows men by their fruits. But there are no fruits where there are no roots, and faith and hope may be in the shade of charity without being starved of all sustenance.

It is instructive to compare and contrast what Arnold and Braithwaite say about morality and religion with Professor C. D. Broad's remarks in *The Mind and its Place in Nature* (pp. 511–12) about the political use of myths and fictions. Broad agrees with Plato that there are certain beliefs, of which he gives a belief in the immortality of the human soul as an example, which ought to be propagated by governments whether they are in fact true or false, on the ground that they are valuable instruments for the promotion of good conduct on the part of the mass of the population. Broad is quite explicit about his motives. Arnold is clearly but inexplicitly impelled by similar motives. Braithwaite's position is more complicated. He neither, like Arnold, wholly rejects certain beliefs because they are false, nor, like Broad, recommends that they should be propagated in spite of being false. He is prepared to tolerate their *use* as stimuli to moral action, and regards questions of their truth or falsehood as subsidiary and incidental. Would he be happy to countenance the widespread use of *astrological* stories to reinforce behaviour policies, regardless of whether there is in fact any scientific basis for astrology?

Braithwaite's account is extreme and unorthodox, and his own protestations to the contrary have a half-hearted air. But there is no doubt that some of its ingredients may be found in a weaker solution in more orthodox circles, and Braithwaite is able to quote in his own support a passage from the *Report of the Church of England's Commission on Doctrine*, published in 1938: 'Statements affirming particular facts may be found to have value as pictorial expressions of spiritual truths, even though the supposed facts themselves did not actually happen. It is not therefore of necessity illegitimate to accept and affirm particular clauses of the Creeds while understanding them in this symbolic sense.'

But the Commissioners are still concerned with spiritual *truths*. The title of this section of their Report is 'On the Application to the Creeds of the Conception of Symbolic Truth'. We are still concerned with continuities, with matters of degree, and Braithwaite is as far from orthodoxy as some forms of orthodoxy are from fundamentalism. He draws a sharp distinction between 'unsophisticated Christians', who accept the traditional stories of cosmogony and eschatology, and 'educated Christians' like himself:

> Educated Christians of the present day who attach importance to the doctrine of the Atonement certainly do not believe an empirically testable story in Matthew Arnold's or any other form. But it is the fact that entertainment in thought of this and other Christian stories forms the context in which Christian resolutions are made which serves to distinguish Christian assertions from those made by adherents of another religion, or of no religion.   (p. 26)

The distinction has become so sharp that a stage has been reached where the education and the sophistication have swallowed up the Christianity. The orthodox case against Braithwaite is at its most pointed in these two questions: (1) Can there be *heresy* if there is no orthodoxy, no insistence on the *truth* of any *doctrine*? (2) Can there be theology without the possibility of heresy?

'I am the Way, the Truth and the Life.' The orthodox and traditional interpretation of this saying insists on the fundamental priority of the Truth. It is because Christianity claims to offer the *truth* about the nature of the world and man and God and Christ that it requires and expects of men that they should follow a particular Way and live a particular Life. Braithwaite puts the carriage before the pair when he use formulations of Christian truth merely as means of expressing a resolution to follow the Christian way and to live the Christian life.

Braithwaite reveals here again his allegiance to positivistic and reductionist modes of thought which have led to similar mistakes in parallel cases. Professor C. L. Stevenson, in his paper on 'Ethical Judgments and Avoidability' (*Mind*, 1938) identifies free human actions with those that are capable of being influenced by persuasion, advice, reward, punishment, praise or blame. He reduces freedom to a capability of being influenced in these ways. But this again is to put the cart before the horse. It is certainly true that a free action is one that is subject to these influences, but it is because it is free that it can be so influenced, and not because it can be so influenced that it is free.

A similar manœuvre is performed again, by Stevenson and others, when they give an emotivist account of the nature of moral judgements. They identify the judgement that something is good with the judgement that it is approved of, or with the expression or evincing or evoking of such approval. But this is no more legitimate than to identify the claim that a proposition is *true* with the claim that it is *believed*, or with the expression or evincing or evoking of such belief. It would certainly be paradoxical for a man to say that something is good but that he does not approve of it, or that he approves of something but that it is not good, but the paradox is on all fours with that of saying that something is true but that one does not believe it, or that one believes something but that it is not true. And in both cases the order of priority is the same. We hope that we shall believe only what is true, and we ought equally to hope that we shall approve only of what is good.

Arnold and Braithwaite are like the shopkeeper who is out of stock, who cannot supply what we came in to buy, but who has something else to offer that is 'just as good – in fact, better'. They recognize that traditional religion is widely rejected as false, and they themselves believe that it *is* false. Instead of saying this in set terms they offer us something else, which they purport to identify with traditional religion, which they parcel up in the wrappings of traditional religion, which they find more acceptable and which they expect to be more acceptable to others.

I believe that they are gravely mistaken in their accounts of the nature of religion, and in particular of the Christian religion, but they do have the great merit of making open and explicit some motives and trains of thought which are too often obscure and inexplicit in the works of more pious and supposedly more orthodox writers. Arnold says in the Preface to the popular edition of *Literature and Dogma* that 'lucidity is a condition from which the theology of the future cannot escape'. Arnold and Braithwaite have achieved their lucidity only at the cost of jettisoning theology, but we must nevertheless be grateful for the lucidity and for the help it can give us in our own efforts to present what they misrepresent. At least their misrepresentations are not fraudulent like those of some who turn from lucidity to the comfortable darkness of unreason.

6 · Foundations

This catalogue of criticism and denial may reasonably give rise to the question, 'What then is the *true* account of the matter?' I have followed a negative way. I have rejected most of the most familiar accounts of the logical nature of theological and in particular of Christian affirmation and belief. It would be natural to expect me now to offer a positive view, to try to be constructive after all the destructive criticism.

This is a challenge that I accept subject only to some fairly strict limitations, since I suggest, contrary to what is implied by the terms of the challenge, that my reasoned criticism of mistaken accounts has itself involved making some positive suggestions about the epistemological character of religion and theology. And I should be contradicting myself if I now undertook to offer a neat set of conclusions, since my purpose has been to show that every such neat account is and must be mistaken, that the nature of theology cannot be set out in any brief compass, in any tidy formula; that the search for *the* analysis of theological propositions is in principle misguided. But what I can and will try to do is to put into a more positive form the results of my critical investigations, and to draw some morals from the position as I have presented it.

My main conclusions are these: (1) Factual claims are indispensable to theology and especially to Christian theology. Christianity is, after all, as we are constantly reminded even by many whose more detailed discussion of it fails to do justice to the fact, a *historical* religion. At its heart is the doctrine of the incarnation of Christ. For a Christian, therefore, the Arnold-Braithwaite road is closed. He must conceive the existence of God in such a way that it makes a difference to what *this* world is like, just as the beauty of a picture must be conceived in such a way that the beauty cannot be present or absent independently of any other properties of the picture. The difference must make a difference. (2) Moral teaching is also indispensable to religion, and in particular to the Christian religion, as Arnold and Braithwaite insist to the point of exaggeration and distortion. It is an essential feature of Christianity that it enjoins a way of life, that it insists, as Arnold said, on the central place of righteousness and charity. (3) It is essential that there should be a connection between the factual claims and the moral claims, and that the order and *direction* of the connection should be rightly conceived. Orthodox Christianity offers a way because it offers a truth. Affirmation of the truth is not to be thought of as a mere means of expressing a commitment and still less as expressing an arbitrary and gratuitous commitment, to the way and the life. This is not to say that for Christian the whole of morality must be totally different from any morality whose ground is wholly secular, but it is necessary that there should be some differences in morality that are grounded in the non-moral *truths* of his religion. Even if the acceptance of the religion requires no external change, even its 'behaviour policies' are practically indistinguishable from those of some secular morality, there must at least be a morally significant change in the motives for which some or all of the prescribed actions are performed, or some morally significant change in the grounds on which they are enjoined upon the believer. It may be that the fact that a certain course of life in accordance with the will of God is offered as an additional ground to the utilitarian grounds on which the newly converted believer has hitherto pursued such a course, or that a motive of charity is substituted for motives of prudence.

If there is no such change, then the alleged transition from a secular to a religious morality will be merely a change in the outward expression of the morality, of no more importance than the substitution of the *poetical commonplace* 'Poseidon is angry' for 'The sea is rough'.

This contrast between linguistic form and logical content is central to what I have tried to say about the nature of theology. The continuous gradations by which the words 'Poseidon is angry' pass from an initial extreme at which they express a full-blooded literal theological belief that *Poseidon* is angry to a final extreme at which they express only the comparatively anaemic and non-theological fact that the sea is angry, can be paralleled in the case of most, if not all, of the

haracteristic utterances of Christian theology. The Creation
.nd the Resurrection, the Ascension and the Virgin Birth, like
he Annunciation and the Assumption, like the visitations of
Athena and Poseidon, may be very differently conceived with-
·ut being differently expressed. The old words are receptive
·o many new meanings.

This range and variety of interpretation presents a dilemma
·r any theologian who defends in modern times an ancient and
raditional doctrine. At one end of the scale, these beliefs are
traightforwardly intelligible, are to be understood in quite
·nparadoxical ways, but are liable to be rejected as being
·lainly false and contrary to the relevant evidence. At the other
nd of the scale, when they have purchased an immunity
·om this kind of refutation, they are liable, even before they
·each the vanishing point of a complete reduction, to be accused
·f being either unintelligible or ungrounded, or of being too
·ague and indefinite to retain any grip on things as they are,
ny firm lines of communication with the rest of our knowledge.
·rofessor Antony Flew is pressing an attack on this front when
·e speaks of 'death by a thousand qualifications' (*New Essays
·n Philosophical Theology*, p. 97).

It is to this dilemma that Arnold and Braithwaite are
·esponding, and the nature and limitations of their responses
·estify to the starkness and importance of the dilemma. Arnold
·imself bears witness to the inadequacy of a policy of timid
·ithdrawal, of merely weakening the doctrinal force of Christian
·eology, or, as he puts it, of *tinkering* with the abstract ideas, and
· is because he is indisposed to tinker that he boldly abandons
·e whole superstructure or substructure of abstractions.

Wisdom's account promises reassurance to the theologian,
·nd performs at least part of what it promises. He widens our
·onception of fact, of reason, of assertion about what is so in
·e actual world. But I have suggested that the reassurance is
·ot permanent and stable. At the end of this road there arises
·nother barrier, the barrier of divine transcendence. Can the
·anscendence of God survive the revolution that has massacred
·s courtiers – transcendent matter, transcendent mind, trans-
·ndent value, transcendent universal forms?

The trial is still in progress, but if I were summing up now I
·ould do so against the accused. The transcendence of God,

like the transcendence of mind and matter, values and univer
sals, has been invoked to answer questions about what i
ultimate, and when such questions are more fully understood and
more clearly expressed they are seen neither to need nor to
allow the traditional forms of transcendentalist answer. Trans
cendental ontology is made plausible only by an epistemologica
misunderstanding, by an unsure grasp of the nature of the
ultimate grounds of our claims to knowledge.

My insistent theme has been that light can be shed on the
central problems of the philosophy of religion only by a con
sideration of the central problems of philosophy as such. The
problem of theological transcendence is a special case of a
general philosophical problem of transcendence, and tha
problem in turn involves all the most fundamental and per
vasive of epistemological concepts: reason, proof, truth; ex
planation, definition and description. Philosophical problem
are problems about the nature of *ultimate* justification, *ultimate*
explanation, *ultimate* definition and description. When we re
flect on the character of the explanations, proofs, definitions and
descriptions that we offer outside philosophy, in mathematics
science, ethics, theology and elsewhere, we are drawn along a
natural and plausible path of reasoning to what seems to be an
inescapable and yet intolerable dilemma.

The first step is to make the innocent and indeed importan
observation that we cannot offer a satisfactory explanation c
something unless we use in the explanation different terms from
those in which we describe or identify the event or phenomenon
that we have undertaken to explain. For example, we cannot b
allowed to explain the redness of a red thing merely by sayin
that it consists of red particles. We cannot normally explain
why a particular drug induces sleep merely by ascribing to it
dormitive or soporific power. But it is also required of a
explanation that it should refer to something that is bette
known or understood than what it purports to explain. T
explain is to connect the less familiar with the more familiar, wit
what has already been explained or could now be explained

We now seem to be clambering along a chain of linke
explanations, like Bradley's chain of facts, in which each lin
needs to be bound to a further link. How then can we eve
reach the ultimate explanation of anything? We seem to b

destined to travel either along an infinite regress or in a vicious circle. At this point it becomes plausible to suggest that we need something which is ultimate, which itself stands in need of no explanation, if we are to be able to offer an explanation of anything else.

The same line of thought is equally common and equally seductive as applied to demonstration and to definition. It is impossible to demonstrate the truth of a conclusion without using as a premise some other proposition that is not now being demonstrated to be true. It is therefore natural to suppose that we need ultimate premises which are themselves undemonstrated and undemonstrable to serve as the starting-points of all demonstration. Similarly, a definition is unsatisfactory unless it is expressed in terms distinct from those in which what is to be defined has been picked out or described. We therefore seem to need indefinable terms which can function as the ultimate starting-points of all definition.

It seems to follow that proof, explanation, definition and description are impossible, since each of them requires a foundation and no such foundation can be provided except by a *fiat* whose arbitrariness would defeat its claim to supply a rational basis for rationality.

To contemplate this predicament is to revisit a scene that we have twice looked on from other angles. We are again face to face with the sceptic for whom every reason is either too weak to yield the conclusion or strong enough to provoke a renewal of the sceptical attack, and with the irrationalist who appeals to the ultimate arbitrariness of all reasoning as a charter of liberation from the bonds of logic.

The philosopher's stone is at the end of the rainbow, and even if we could reach it it would turn to dust in our hands.

I have said that philosophical mistakes are understandable mistakes. The more understandable the mistake, the profounder the misunderstanding, but also the more important the positive truth that the philosopher fears that he will be denying if he recants. The traditional picture of philosophy as a quest for unshakable foundations is a profound misunderstanding, and its distortions arise from an obsessive and exclusive attention to a profound but partial truth.

It is true that we cannot offer an explanation unless we can

refer to something for which no explanation is *at present* re
quired; it is true that a demonstration needs a premise fo
which at present no demonstration is demanded; and it is tru
that we can provide a satisfactory definition only if and whe
there are some other terms that are accepted and understoo
without a definition. But it does not follow, as it has usuall
and plausibly been thought to follow, that there must be ;
specifiable set of inexplicable, undemonstrable, indefinabl
ἀρχαί, *principia*, principles or premises which are the fixe
and ultimate foundations of all explanation, demonstration an
definition. We can see that it does not follow if we consider tw
smaller scale examples which model the structure of proof an
explanation in general and as such.

The *Oxford English Dictionary* is a monoglot dictionary. I
explains English words by means of English words. A ma
cannot learn the meanings of any English words from such ;
dictionary unless there are some English words whose meaning
he knows before he begins to use the dictionary. But there ar
no English words which are *the* words whose meanings he mus
know before he can learn from the dictionary the meanings c
further English words. Every word whose meaning is explaine
in the dictionary is explained in words whose meanings are als
explained in the dictionary. The whole process of learning th
meanings of English words from the dictionary is *non-viciousl*
circular; regressive, but not viciously regressive.

The same lesson can be read more fully and more clearly i
the logic or epistemology of spatial location. I cannot tell yo
where something is unless you already know where somethin
is. I can give you directions for finding the Guildhall only if yo
can already find some other building or some other object t
which I can relate it. We cannot discuss the spatial locatio
of any object unless there are other objects whose location w
do not need to discuss. But anything that we can agree to us
as a landmark or point of reference is something that is itse
locatable by the same procedure; it is something into whose loca
tion somebody else, or you and I on another occasion, mig
need to inquire. And *any* object may be used as a landmar
There are no particular objects or locations which are t
ultimate, fundamental landmarks or base-lines for the locatio
of all other objects. There *could* not be such ultimate landmark

and we do not *need* such landmarks. They are neither necessary nor possible.

Similarly, there need not be, are not, *could* not be, any ultimate ἀρχαί of definition, explanation and demonstration. To recognize this is to weaken one of the most powerful motives for the generation of transcendent substances and ultimate foundations. I believe that the further working out of these reflections will show the impossibility and also the needlessness of an appeal to transcendence as a solution for the main problems of metaphysics and epistemology. Do similar reflections hold out the hope or the fear of banishing the concept of transcendence from theology? This is a special and specially intractable form of the problem of transcendence, and even a philosopher who was satisfied that all or most other transcendentalist doctrines arose from epistemological misunderstandings might argue that there must be a transcendent God, an ultimate, infinite ground of finite, contingent being.

The lessons of the simpler cases can most fruitfully be applied to this uniquely perplexing case if we consider it in the form of the question, 'Why is there something rather than nothing?' This question is a plea for an ultimate and comprehensive explanation of the universe, for a single substance or principle whose existence or nature will explain why *everything* is as it is.

This question cannot be escaped by saying that it is unreal or illegitimate. It is an expression of genuine puzzlement, of a widely and deeply felt perplexity. It calls for an answer, even if the answer may not take the form that the form of the question seems to expect. The answer may be that the question evinces a misunderstanding; but such an answer will be an answer, and it will be a satisfactory answer if its fuller development explains the nature of the misunderstanding in a way that is calculated to remove the puzzlement that the question expresses. And this is a requirement that must be met even by an answer that does conform to the terms in which the question is framed. The question cannot be answered by saying that God is the explanation of why things are as they are, since this leads to a recurrence of the problem in a new form and at a new level. The riddle can be posed again as a riddle about why there is God-and-the-universe.

Nor will it do to resort to talk of mystery and the

inexpressible. The inscrutably and ineffably mysterious canno
either support or contradict any particular doctrine. Only wha
is articulable and intelligible can enter into logical relations
Substitutes for reason will not answer the problems of th
reason. A brick wall is an opaque obstacle, and what we nee
is a path or a window.

A clue to such understanding as we can at present achieve in
this area is provided by those who wrongly dismiss question
about ultimate cosmic explanation as meaningless. What the
primarily have in mind is that when we speak of the univers
as a whole we are necessarily barred from relating it to any
thing outside or beyond itself, and that therefore the notion c
explanation cannot apply to *everything* as it applies to parts o
aspects of the universe, and in general to particular things o
events, whose explanation is given if at all by relating them t
other and distinct things and events. But to show that th
notion of explanation does not apply here as it applies else
where is not to show that it has *no* application here. Explanation
and modes of explanation, like instances and modes of know
ledge, truth and reason, form a family. Besides causal explana
tion there is also the distinct sense of explanation in which w
explain (or expound, or explicate – *unfold*) a proof, an argumen
a play, a picture. Even here we usually rely in our explana
tion on comparisons and contrasts between what we ar
explaining and other things distinct from and external to it: w
explain by a 'method of parallels' (Wisdom). Usually, but no
always or necessarily. For we may legitimately and usefull
explain a large-scale and complex argument or book or musica
or artistic composition by an *internal* process of relating parts t
each other and to the whole, without necessarily or at ever
point making reference to other arguments or books or com
positions. (This mode of explanation best fits the etymology c
both 'explain' and 'explicate', since here we lay out or unfol
what we wish to be more clearly and fully seen.)

This mode of explanation applies to the world or univers
as a whole as much as to its separate parts or aspects. If it wer
not so, *scientific* cosmology, and not only philosophical an
theological cosmology, would be impossible. And in phil
sophical or theological cosmology, just as in scientific co
mology or in the exposition of *Hamlet* or the *Republic*, the whol

may be illuminated by comparison or analogy with one of its own parts. *Comparison* is necessary to explanation, but it need not be comparison of the whole of the *explicandum* with something wholly distinct from and external to it.

We must not be distracted here by questions about the correctness or incorrectness of particular essays in such a style of explanation. It could not be misconducted if it could not be conducted at all, and in such a work as Hume's *Dialogues Concerning Natural Religion* it is attempted in a form in which it can be understood and criticized. Indeed the work consists of conversations in which we are given both the attempts and some of the necessary criticisms. The idea that the world is or is like a machine, or an animal, or a vegetable, is supported and opposed by comparing the world with some of its parts, including machines, animals and vegetables.

The consideration of the world as a whole no more requires reference to something external to the world as a whole than the consideration of physical space requires something external to the set of spatial relations between the particular objects and positions in space. The rejection of absolute space is an instructive precedent for the rejection of absolute logical space. The supposition that there must be ultimate foundations for knowledge and reasoning is comparable with the idea that the possibility of locating objects in space requires as an external frame of reference some base lines or landmarks which under-write the whole system of spatial relations without themselves being locatable within the system.

Wisdom shows, in 'Gods' and elsewhere, that we do not need and cannot have something external to the world-as-a-whole to which we can relate or compare the world. He implies but does not say that the survival of theology does not require the assumption or conclusion that there is such an external ground or source. I have suggested that the language of traditional theology cannot be dissociated from such an assumption or conclusion without being converted to uses too far from the traditional uses to qualify as re-expressions of traditional beliefs.

These are only hints and guesses,
Hints followed by guesses.

T. S. Eliot, *Four Quartets*, p. 33

But though I cannot here and now do more to articulate these hints and to confirm these guesses, I hope that at least I have given good reasons for supposing that we need not and must not, in this or any area of philosophical or theological inquiry, remain content with hints and guesses. If my guesses are not right, then they must be wrong. If my hints are inarticulate, they are articulable, and to articulate them would be to make them more useful or to show that and why they must be useless.

Wisdom shows that we do not need and cannot have the external frame of reference that we have craved as a possible and necessary and sufficient condition of our understanding of our place in the scheme of things, and of our questionable confidence that there is a *scheme* of things. He hints that theology can survive this recognition. I guess that traditional theology is so wedded to what Wisdom rightly leads us to reject that whatever survives the recognition will no longer be theology.

But we need not wait for an answer to the ultimate cosmic riddle before we recognize that even it must have an answer. It is the subject of controversy. There are rival answers to it, and competing ways of trying to show that it is misconceived and cannot have an answer tailored to fit the form of the question. These conditions, which are so often made to look like grounds for sceptical retreat, are a guarantee that there is scope for progress in understanding. Where there is conflict, somebody is wrong; and where it can be known that somebody is wrong it is possible and necessary to hope and try to find out who is right. Even in the most knotted tangle of mystery and perplexity there is objectivity because there is inquiry.

And we must not allow a preoccupation with this fundamental crux to distract us from wider and hardly less profound considerations. The belief in a transcendent ground of all things, whether or not it is central and indispensable to theology, is only a part of theology. We must keep in view the variety and multiplicity of the other elements of which theology is composed, and the extent to which they criss-cross and overlap both with each other and with much that lies outside theology. Morality, history and psychology, biological and cosmological speculation, and every mode or medium in which we may seek for an understanding of the nature of man and life and the world, for a perspective on human nature and human history and their wider setting, can be found both within theology and outside it. They all remain available as elements in theology which, even in their religious forms, are accessible and valuable to many who reject the claim of religion to offer an authoritative and comprehensive truth. To exclude them from the scope of religion or to regard them as forming no part of the essence of religion because they can also be found in isolation from religion, would be to commit the fallacy against which I have so often inveighed: the fallacy of supposing that only what is either necessary or sufficient for the application of a term is relevant to its application.

It is because all these elements *are* ingredients of religion that Arnold and Braithwaite can plausibly present as religion something that consists only of these elements.

Once again we have something to learn from the simple pieties of Homer and Sophocles. We have seen that we can still learn from the plays and poems of the ancient Greeks, although we reject the basis of the mythological structure through which they express their insight and their understanding. The myths continue to teach us something because they are attached to, and grounded in, an experience that we share. It would therefore be astonishing if the Christian religion, whether when considered as a united and comprehensive body of doctrine it is true or false, did not contain much knowledge and truth, much understanding and insight, that remain available and accessible even to those who reject its doctrinal foundations. In and through Christianity the thinkers and writers and painters and moralists of two thousand years have struggled to make sense of life and the world and men. They have not struggled in vain. And they were struggling to find, not to fashion; to see how things are, not to mould them to a heart's desire. What is more, the life that they wrestled with is *our* life; the world they have portrayed is the world that *we* live in; the men that they were striving to understand are ourselves.

We may add to this two points that I have stressed throughout this inquiry: (1) the variety and multiplicity of *essentially* theological beliefs, such as a belief in the Incarnation, and the Trinity, and the Resurrection, Atonement, Grace and Immortality – a range of doctrines too various to be covered

by any single neat account of the nature of theological propositions; (2) the variety of possible interpretations of each of these
doctrines taken separately, the fact that each of them is as
Protean as a belief in Poseidon or Athena. It then becomes clear
how unsatisfactory it is to speak of accepting or rejecting
Christianity *as a whole*. There are too many separate elements in
Christian doctrine, each of which raises too many separate
questions, each of which is capable of too many distinguish-
able interpretations, for a man to be able to reveal very much
of the nature of his beliefs and allegiances by saying a simple
Yes or a simple No to the superficially simple, single question,
'Is Christianity true, or is it false?'

In this respect religion is closely parallel with politics. It is
a commonplace of politics that all parties are coalitions. A
man may disagree with this or that particular element in the
policy of the Conservative Party and yet have an unquestionable claim to call himself a loyal and convinced Conservative.
A man may agree with a considerable number of elements in
the policy of the Conservative Party and yet have an unquestionable right not to call himself a loyal and convinced
Conservative. The issues are too many and too various, and
many of them are too independent of too many others, for the
situation to be one in which a simple Yes or a simple No is
appropriate, for it to be a simple matter of 'we' and 'they',
those who are for us and those who are against us. And there is
the separate and additional but connected point that the policy
of a political party may legitimately be different at different
times and in different circumstances.

T. E. Hulme was oversimplifying the matter when he said
that the point of all creeds and manifestos is to draw 'a pecu-
liarly complicated but quite definite line which will mark
you off finally and distinctly from the people you can't stand'.
Is the drawing of such sharp lines appropriate in religion? A
strict orthodoxy must say that it is, and even the most moderate
adherent of a religious doctrine, so long as it *is* a *doctrine*,
must draw the line somewhere.

Whatever ought to be the case, it is clear that in fact every
church and every sect and every congregation is as much a
coalition as every political party. And every congregation of
humanists or heretics or members of the Rationalist Press

Association is also a coalition. Every church, and every band of heretics, may contain its Homer and its Euripides, its wise men and its shepherds; it may range from Athanasius to Arnold, from Bunyan to Braithwaite. Some of this diversity may be found even in the mind of the individual believer or unbeliever, especially if he is reflective about his faith or lack of faith. Every man is his own coalition.

To see all this is to cease to seek clear-cut criteria for distinguishing Christians from non-Christians. There are no religious acid-tests. The class of sincere Christians, like the class of games or instances of knowledge, has a complex internal structure and indefinite boundaries. Its members may vary widely and in many dimensions and yet all remain within those boundaries. 'In my Father's house are many mansions.' But an indefinite boundary is still a boundary, and a boundary that may be crossed. There are limits to religious liberalism, and on the far side of them there is ample liberty but no religion. A man may travel step by slow step and yet travel so far from the central affirmations of what he claims to be his religion that his claim can no longer be accepted.

An awareness of these same complexities is also relevant and indispensable to the treatment of the question 'What is the nature of the *mistake* of the believer or of the unbeliever?' If there is such a thing as religious truth then there is such a thing as religious falsehood, and either the believer or the unbeliever is under a misapprehension. Either the believer sees what is not there to be seen or the unbeliever fails to see what is there to be seen. What is the nature of this misapprehension? Is it a failure of the will or of the understanding? What role, if any, can the emotions legitimately play in religious inquiry? These questions call urgently for an answer from one who explicitly insists, as I have insisted, that religious questions are objectively determinable, that theology is a branch of knowledge. But they arise for all Christians and for most non-Christians, since to engage in inquiry or dispute about religion at all, to accept or reject any religious view, is implicitly to recognize that in religion as elsewhere there are rights and wrongs and truths and falsehoods.

These questions belong to pure philosophy, to the philosophy of theology and not to philosophical theology. They are questions about the nature and mode of justification of theological propositions, and as such are logically independent of any question about the truth or falsehood of this or that particular religious or anti-religious view. Disputes about them cut across the lines of division between theists and atheists, Christians and rationalists or humanists. The theist who emphasizes the importance of an element of will or choice in religious faith may be echoed by the atheist who sees religious belief as wilful and religious thinking as wishful.

In religion as in other inquiries it is a proper awareness of the multiplicity and complexity of the issues that gives rise to such talk of decision or choice, of unreasoned prejudice or arbitrary commitment. Wherever there is great complexity there is a craving for simplicity, and when a question is too intricate to have a simple answer that will do justice to all the relevant facts and circumstances it becomes tempting to seek simplicity in another dimension; to abandon the search for a complex answer that will match the complexities of the question and its subject matter, and to talk instead of the need for a simple choice, to authorize the exercise of an option that is not subject to the constraints of argument and evidence.

The road to commitment is not the only route along which men have tried to escape from the tangled forest of religious perplexity. Some have taken comfort in the thought that our temperaments or emotional dispositions determine our religious views, and that they are turning away from thinking not because it is laborious but because it is vain. A man who sets bounds to reason tends to place them suspiciously near to the limits of his own understanding.

The will to believe and the heart's reasons are not tied by philosophical patents. They are the common currency of religious discussion. It has become a commonplace to say that nobody is ever reasoned into or out of a religion, that nobody ever becomes a Christian or an atheist as a result of argument or discussion. The popular evangelist calls upon his hearers to *decide* for Christ.

The same pattern recurs in every sphere in which there are problems of great but informal complexity. We are repeatedly told that in morals and politics we cannot in principle aspire to find out what *is* right, what *is* good, what *is* true, but must simply choose. It is said that nobody ever joins or leaves a political party as a result of argument or evidence; that philosophical discussion is a charade in which the so-called reasons and proofs are a fancy dress designed to disguise mere differences of temperament; that our judgements of the characters and personalities of our friends and enemies are based on emotion and prejudice, and therefore cannot be altered by any appeal to the understanding.

These ideas are all delusions, and most of them are dangerous delusions.

It is true that dramatic conversions are rare. It seldom happens that a man changes his opinion on a political or moral or philosophical or religious issue as the immediate and direct result of reading a book or hearing a lecture or taking part in a conversation. But to conclude from this that books and lectures and conversations make no difference is to fall into the mistake of the child who thinks he is not growing because his measured height this morning is the same as it was yesterday afternoon. Argument and reasoning do change people's views, but they usually do so gradually and undramatically. As the child imperceptibly grows taller he also grows in knowledge and understanding, and much of this intellectual growth is also undramatic and imperceptible.

Much is made of the fact that we often spend hours in vigorous discussion of a philosophical problem, a political crisis, or the character of a friend or enemy, and still must 'agree to differ' because each of us continues to express his overall view in the form of words in which he first declared it. Once again we need to remember that an unchanged form of words may mask a change of content, and that a man's view of a complex scene or subject may be radically transformed by stages each of which is too slight when taken by itself to call for a revision of the label or banner under which he conceals the variegated detail of his knowledge and ignorance.

The power of great complexity to freeze the understanding and to puzzle the will is familiar from many contexts outside philosophy and religion. The intricacies of foreign policy, or the laws of England, or international finance, or textual criticism, may leave the layman baffled to know how anybody can find his way through any part of the maze. But while nobody understands every twist and turn of all the pathways, it is clear to us on reflection that a Bevin or a Maitland or a Keynes or a Housman has a degree of grasp that we lack, but which is denied to us by contingent limitations in our powers and our experience and not by the barrier of any logical principle. The more difficult and complicated a matter is, the greater is the need for persistence and determination in the application of the human reason to it. To despair of making any further progress in such fields is always to underestimate the amount of progress that has been made, and to succumb to the sceptical confusion of supposing that we cannot know anything until we know everything. It is usually also to be deceived by a false perspective in which the most difficult and contentious questions in the foreground are allowed to hide the background of agreement against which we can and must continue to seek answers to them.

The cases that come before the courts are usually difficult and controversial. That is why they come before the courts. But the settled cases of the past not only help to settle the unsettled issue that is now before the court: they also make it unnecessary to trouble the court with what can be disposed of by counsel's opinion, the word of an experienced solicitor, or the informed common sense of the lay client himself. There can be no trial where there is no *res judicata*. A question can be formulated only against a background in which there are signposts pointing towards an answer.

To talk of temperamental differences as the basis of ethical and philosophical and religious disagreement is to change the subject from logic to psychology. We can of course on favoured occasions causally explain why a man believes in ghosts or Free Trade or Papal infallibility. But we can explain equally well why another man is a materialist or a protectionist or a member of the Presbyterian Church of Northern Ireland. What is more, we can explain why one man believes in a flat earth or the possibility of squaring the circle and why another man does not. If to explain were to explain away, to establish that there is no good reason to accept the belief explained, and some good reason against it, we should be able to establish a tissue of contradictions. When we understand the causes of a man's beliefs we may still be in the dark about the reasons for them,

and about whether they are good or bad reasons for a true or
for a false belief.

There is a further and more recondite difficulty that faces
those who scout the objectivity of inquiry into complex and
contentious questions. They seldom notice that the features on
which they rely as indications of the unsettleability of moral
and religious disputes are also to be found in my dispute with
them about whether moral and religious disputes are settleable.
The question 'Does every question have a right answer?' is
itself very like the questions of which it is most commonly and
most plausibly said that they have no right answers. Hence a
dilemma arises for anyone who says that I am mistaken in
giving the answer Yes to the question 'Does every question have
a right answer?' Either he is mistaken in holding that I am
giving a mistaken answer to that question or he is mistaken in
holding that it is not the case that every question has a right
answer.

But the main sources of confusion are a bewilderment in the
face of great and informal complexity, and a craving for
universality and finality that is all the more disastrous for being
combined with a misunderstanding of the nature of universality.
A comparison and contrast between the accounts of moral reflection given by Professor R. M. Hare and M. Jean-Paul Sartre
will show how various are the misapprehensions that may be
traceable to common sources, and how closely similar in
motivation may be philosophical doctrines whose most manifest
tendencies rightly lead us to think of them as radically opposed
on topics that are central to their scope.

Hare insists on finding a necessary role in moral rationality
for universal rules or principles. Sartre stresses the particularity
and individuality of every stubbornly troublesome moral
dilemma or predicament, and represents it as a ground for the
conclusion that there is no moral rationality. We must simply
choose, decide, invent, and no decision in one case can be
brought usefully to bear in favour of a particular decision in any
other case. Hare, too, makes morality in the end a matter of
unreasoned personal choice and commitment, but for him the
commitment is to rules or principles from which we then
deductively derive the answers to our particular perplexities.
Conversely, when we give an answer to any particular moral

question, we are logically committed to a universal principle that requires of us, on pain of inconsistency, that we should give the corresponding answer in every case that also exhibits the features that we cite in giving our reasons for our answer in the given case.

Here again is an occasion for the application of Ramsey's Maxim. Hare and Sartre make the same fundamental mistake: the mistake of supposing that all reasoning, moral or non-moral, requires universal principles. Hare recognizes that there is such a thing as moral reasoning, and since he supposes that reasoning requires universal principles, he misrepresents the nature of moral reasoning in order to find a role in it for such principles. Sartre recognizes that morality does not allow of such principles, but since he too supposes that rationality requires such principles he wrongly concludes that there is no scope for reasoning about morals.

In theology, too, it is easy to suppose that because the kind of reasoning that is appropriate does not fit this or that grossly distorted pattern or paradigm, it does not qualify as reasoning at all, or alternatively that it must be misrepresented as fitting patterns or paradigms that it does not fit. The more fully we explore the character of morality and theology and the character of the most seductive misunderstandings of their character, the more confirmation we find for a gloomy conclusion that needs no confirmation, but which may strike us with new force against the background of these reflections; that in thinking, or in failing adequately to think, about questions of morality or theology or politics or philosophy of life, there is infinite and inexhaustible scope for over-simplification, for mystification, confusion and unclarity, and, perhaps still worse, for laziness, evasion, self-deception and hypocrisy: for a whole range of failures of moral integrity compounded by consciously or unconsciously fraudulent reliance on philosophical sophistries and illusions.

7 · Proverbs

In discussing the nature of knowledge in general, and the place on the map of knowledge that belongs to theology and religion, I have offered an implicit answer to the first of the two familiar complaints against contemporary philosophy, to the charge that it neglects those large questions about the scope and limits of human knowledge which used to preoccupy the metaphysical philosophers of the past. I now turn to the second challenge, to the accusation that contemporary philosophers ignore, and are required by their epistemological principles to ignore, the questions about human life and human happiness, about the philosophy of life and conduct, which were also within the province of the great philosophers of the past.

These two themes are connected, because teaching about human life and conduct is an important element in religion, so important that many thinkers, including Arnold and Braithwaite, have sought to identify it with religion. I have urged strong objections against the accounts offered by Arnold and Braithwaite in so far as they purport to be accounts of theology and religion in general and of Christianity in particular. They are seriously incomplete, since they identify one part of religion and theology with the whole of religion and theology. They underestimate the variety of the elements that together compose theology and religion, and the criss-crossings and over-lappings that connect those elements with other inquiries and activities that are properly excluded from religion and theology. They also misrepresent the nature of Christian theology by falsifying the order of priority between Christian teaching about life and conduct and Christian teaching about the nature of man and the world and God. Orthodox Christianity claims to offer the way and the life because if offers the truth. Arnold and Braithwaite use the formulae of Christian doctrine as mere means of expressing a commitment to the Christian way and

the Christian life. They convert the proposition that God is
Love into the proposition that Love is God.

It is a further objection to this type of account, especially in
its more extreme forms, that it cannot accommodate the claim
of orthodox Christianity to a unique and exclusive truth and
validity. When such liberty of interpretation is exercised that
Christian formulae are used as statements of policy or declara-
tions of intention, and not as making any *assertions*, any claim
to express *the truth*, it becomes possible to represent Christianity
as compatible with other religious and non-religious outlooks
which must, on any orthodox interpretation, be recognized as
heresies and rejected as incompatible with the truth of Christian
doctrine. There is also the related but separate difficulty
that this type of account makes it possible for the function
that it attributes to religion, or to a particular set of religious
doctrines, to be fulfilled by other and non-religious modes of
thought. If religion is reduced to reflection about human life
and human action, then it ceases to be identifiable as something
with its own characteristic function and field of operation.
There are other and recognizably non-religious media in which
reflection about human life and human action can be effectively conducted and expressed.

In pressing these and other objections against Arnold
and Braithwaite's epistemological accounts of religion and
theology, and against their claim that what they are explaining
and defending is *Christianity*, stripped only of some inessential
encumbrances, I have not suggested, and I do not now wish to
suggest, that what they have done in the name of Christianity
is in itself objectionable. I can reject their claim to be Christian
without rejecting their claim to be doing valuable thinking
about human life and conduct, and *a fortiori* without suggesting
that there is no scope for or possibility of doing valuable thinking about human life and conduct. When they call themselves
Christians they misrepresent both Christianity and their own
reflection, but they are right in thinking that such reflection is
important and that it can be effective.

Such reflection can be effectively conducted both inside and
outside the confines of religion. It can even be effectively
conducted inside the otherwise empty shell of religion, as it
is conducted by Arnold and Braithwaite themselves. The fact

hat so much valuable thinking of this kind has been done with-
n the Christian tradition and in Christian terms and categories
s one considerable motive for continuing to try to do it under
hose auspices; for trying to do it with the help of the Christian
stories' that are Braithwaite's own chosen instruments for the
ask. There is a vast storehouse of thought and experience that
as been formed in and expressed through the terms of the
Christian theological tradition. The doors of the storehouse
emain open even to those who have rejected the doctrinal
oundation on which it was built. And this is what Arnold has
n mind when, once again using the language of traditional
nd even evangelical orthodoxy, he urges us to 'try it' and
romises that 'it works'.

It would be surprising if Christian theology did not retain
his function for non-Christians, for unbelievers like Arnold and
Braithwaite, since even Greek religion and mythology retain a
imilar value as a language for reflection about man and life
nd the world, although nobody now believes in the literal truth
f the propositions about the world, and about the gods of the
antheon, that were for Homer and his contemporaries the
oundation of their storehouse of thought and experience.

When I set aside my dispute with Arnold and Braithwaite
bout their claim to be Christians and Christian theologians,
nd join them in examining and defending the kind of thinking
bout life and its problems that they have preached and
ractised, new questions at once arise. What is the nature and
cope of such thinking? In what terms is it to be conducted?
How can it be effective? What, if anything, can recent philo-
ophy contribute to the progress of such thinking, and to the
nderstanding of its nature? Where do religion and theology
tand if their dogmas and doctrines are removed, if their
ommerce with the transcendent is under blockade, and only
he philosophy of life and conduct is left? Are religious terms
nd categories necessary to the conduct of the philosophy of
ife, or to its effective conduct? What other media, if any, are
vailable for this kind of thinking?

These questions cannot be answered without giving some
ccount of moral knowledge and moral thinking, partly for the
bvious reason that any inquiry that could properly be called
hilosophy of life would necessarily include morality within its

scope, but partly for two less obvious and more controversial reasons: first, that though philosophy of life includes morality and moral reflection, it is not confined to or exhausted by morality; secondly, that there are a number of misunderstandings about the nature of morality which have recurred again and again in the history of moral philosophy, which are prominent in the writings of the most fashionable moral philosophers of today, and which are especially liable to misrepresent the nature and to inhibit the progress of philosophy of life.

To speak of moral *knowledge* is already to be in conflict with many contemporary moral philosophers, according to whom morality is a matter of choice, decision, intention and commitment, and allows no scope for discovery, knowledge, truth and falsehood. Since these misrepresentations of the nature of moral reasoning are themselves among the main causes of the neglect of philosophical thinking about substantive questions of morals and politics and philosophy of life, and since they also, in a manner characteristic of philosophical misunderstandings, draw valuable attention to some of the leading features of what they misdescribe, it will be useful to consider them at least in outline.

A subjectivist or sceptical account of morality may arise from any one of a number of different sources, and its virtues and defects will vary according to its genesis and motivation. The first, and from the metaphysical point of view the most important source, is the epistemological motive of emphasizing the contrasts between moral knowledge and some of the other main kinds of knowledge. The moral sceptic, like the sceptic of the senses, perceives differences of logical kind between one species of knowledge and another, and then, under the influence of a misplaced craving for unity, simplicity and generality, under the impression that the instances of knowledge must all conform to a single pattern or paradigm, concludes that the two species are *too* different to belong to the same kind, that one of them must be denied its title to be a kind of knowledge at all. The sceptic of the senses denies that there can be knowledge of the material world because he notices that propositions about material things have neither the necessity of propositions of mathematics and logic nor the incorrigibility of propositions about my immediate present sensations. The moral sceptic denies that there can be knowledge of right and wrong because he notices that our feelings and personal responses are involved in the most characteristic moral judgements in ways in which they are not involved in the most typical logical and factual judgements. Both sceptics misrepresent an internal variety among the instances of a single kind as being a division between two or more distinct kinds.

One phrase that occurs repeatedly in sceptical argumentation is a useful indication of the nature of sceptical mistakes. We are told that we cannot establish moral propositions to be true *as* we can establish mathematical or scientific propositions to be true, just as we are told by the sceptic of the senses that we do not know propositions about the external world *in the way that* we know propositions of mathematics or propositions about our immediate experience. These forms of expression are seriously ambiguous, and the diagnosis and correction of the ambiguity helps to identify for us the sources of sceptical misrepresentations.

This point can be made clearer if it is considered in connection with a simple non-philosophical example. I may say to one person on one occasion that my son does not play the violin, as my daughter does. I may say to another person on another occasion that my daughter does not play the violin as Yehudi Menuhin does. Though I use the same form of expression (apart from the all-important comma) my point is entirely different on the two occasions. On the first occasion I am saying that my daughter does play the violin, and that my son does not. On the second occasion I am not saying that my daughter does not play the violin and that Yehudi Menuhin does, but that between the violin playing of my daughter and that of Yehudi Menuhin there are great differences of technique and quality.

When somebody says that we do not know propositions of one kind *as* we know, or *in the way that* we know, propositions of another kind, it is important that he and we should be clear whether he wishes to say that propositions of the first kind cannot be known at all, or that the way in which they are known is different from the way in which propositions of the second kind are known. It is characteristic of philosophical sceptics in general, and of moral sceptics in particular, that they put forward arguments which do support a conclusion of the second kind while claiming to support a conclusion of the first kind.

In specifying further what they take to be the point of contrast between moral inquiry and factual inquiry, moral sceptics often say that there is nothing in the world to which my moral judgement must correspond in order to be correct or well founded in the way that my remarks on matters of fact must correspond to how the world is if they are to be true. Here we see the influence of what I have elsewhere called 'the idea that objectivity requires an object'. The sceptic shares with some of the objectivists and intuitionists who are his most violent opponents the mistaken idea that there is no objective inquiry where there is no set of objects whose qualities and relations are being investigated. Both parties in this dispute think that morality cannot be allowed to be objective unless it consists in the investigation or inspection of a transcendent world of moral values. The sceptic denies the objectivity because he rightly wishes to deny the existence of the objects. The transcendentalist concludes that there must be such objects because he rightly wishes to defend the objectivity.

The motives and alleged grounds of moral scepticism are seldom purely epistemological. Defenders of subjective and emotive and prescriptive theories of ethics are usually prompted also by a *moral* motive which some of them recognize and openly acknowledge: a liberal or individualist outlook and a fear of moral dogmatism and authoritarianism. They are afraid that a recognition of the objectivity of moral inquiry, an admission that there is such a thing as moral knowledge, will lead to tyranny and inquisition. Professor P. H. Nowell-Smith gives typical expression to this anxiety when he remarks that 'it is no accident that religious persecutions are the monopoly of objective theorists' (*Ethics*, p. 47). Professor Hare writes in *Freedom and Reason* (p. 2) that 'we are free to form our own moral opinions in a much stronger sense' than the sense in which we are free to form our own opinions on questions of scientific fact. Mr Alan Montefiore (*Proc. Arist. Soc. Supp.*, 1961) is so concerned to arrive at conclusions on moral philosophy that will square with his 'individualism' that he seems almost to include the individualism among his premises.

I hope soon to set out elsewhere the full reasons why these anxieties seem to me to be misplaced, and to reconcile their reasonable concern for freedom, integrity and authenticity with the rationality and objectivity that belong to moral reflection. The most important step is to draw a clear distinction between the *voluntary* and the *arbitrary*, on lines suggested by Kant's remarks on moral freedom in *Religion within the Limits of Reason Alone*. He shows that the fact that 'freedom is absolutely required' for the adoption of a religious faith, *logically* required for the adoption to *be* the adoption of a *religious faith*, is quite compatible with the objectivity of the question whether the content of that faith is true or false. Similarly, there may be two people each of whom in all sincerity and authenticity answers a moral question in a way that *contradicts* the other's answer: in such a case, as in every case of a dispute in which one man contradicts another, at most one of the parties can be right and at least one of them is wrong.

What should perhaps be singled out as a third distinct source of moral scepticism, though in the work of most sceptics it is thickly intertwined with one or both of the other two strands, is a properly keen awareness of the difficulty, the complexity, and the consequent contentiousness, of most of our serious moral perplexities. This is specially dangerous when it is combined, as it usually is, with the idea that to answer a moral question is to bring to bear on it universal principles or criteria from which the answer in the particular case may be deductively derived. Aristotle has been praised and blamed for what is thought to be an element of subjectivism in his remark that ethics is concerned with 'what is only for the most part so'. But Aristotle's own analogy with the art of healing shows that his recognition of complexity and relativity carries no such consequence. Medical schools cannot instil into their students a set of unexceptionable rules for prescribing pills and potions to of all sorts and conditions of men; but with the use of a skilled judgement the doctor may hope to find the right dose of the right drug for this or that particular patient, and there is no logical barrier to his finding the right dose for every patient.

It is not an accident that one way of disorganizing a railway system or a factory is to 'work to rule', to apply the book without any saving judgement or common sense.

Whatever its sources and grounds on particular occasions, moral scepticism of any variety may be inhibiting to first-order moral reflection, so that here is at least one place where metaphysical inquiry may have results that are of practical non-metaphysical interest. But it would be easy to exaggerate the inhibiting effect of philosophical scepticism on primary moral reflection. The case is closely similar to that of scepticism of the senses, which notoriously does not lead to the difficulties or hesitations in first-order dealings with the external world that we might expect it to produce. The parallel is close in another respect. Moral scepticism, like scepticism of the senses, is a paradoxical doctrine. It is as contrary to common sense, as much in conflict with common usage, as solipsism, or scepticism about the future or the past, or any other metaphysical sceptical theory, and as such it is open to the mode of refutation that Moore used against sensory scepticism in his 'Proof of an External World'. It is a mark of the power of the motives I have considered that so many contemporary philosophers who are well satisfied with Moore's proof of an external world, or with something closely analogous to it, and therefore with a common-sense account of perception and our knowledge of material things, continue to maintain what is in effect a sceptical view about morality, in spite of the fact that a proof of the objectivity of morals can be produced which is valid by parity of reasoning with Moore's proof of an external world. What has been called 'Moore's paradox' applies to this case as strikingly as to the case of scepticism about material things. Here too philosophers defend theses which are incompatible with what they themsevles, as reflective moral agents and judges, *know* to be true.

The formal theories of many contemporary philosophers of morals require them to regard as misuses of language many of the most familiar and natural of our common uses of words. In the film of Alan Sillitoe's *Saturday Night and Sunday Morning* there is a scene where the hero's mistress turns on him in a quarrel and says, 'You never know the difference between right and wrong.' The words are so ordinary and natural that it seems doubtful whether any moral philosopher, whatever his theory, can have felt as he read the book or saw the film that language was being misused. And this is not an odd or isolated instance from ordinary language. We commonly do use in moral contexts all the epistemic expressions that we commonly use in non-moral contexts. We use in and of moral reflection all the expressions that we also use in and of reflection on non-moral questions. The list is far too long to set out here in full, but a small selection is sufficient to underline the main lesson that common sense and common language do not support those philosophers who dig deep gulfs or erect high barriers between facts and values: ignorance and knowledge, argument, judgement, opinion, reasons and conclusions, thinking, wondering, finding out, realizing, discovering, recognizing – all these concepts and all their close kindred are as much at home in morality as in any other mode of inquiry or investigation.

To recognize the possibility of moral knowledge is also to recognize the importance of pursuing it, and therefore to overcome one of the main obstacles to effort and progress in one department of what I have called philosophy of life. But philosophy of life is wider in scope than the pursuit of moral knowledge, even when moral knowledge is sufficiently widely understood, and is not confined to a concern with action and choice. That these concepts are centrally important in morality may explain but it does not justify the myopia that sees them as the whole of morality, to the exclusion of the concepts of discovery and insight and knowledge.

In a discussion in Cambridge some years ago Professor Stuart Hampshire made some remarks that typify the limitation of outlook that I am here opposing. He said that the modern reader finds the moral world of the Homeric poems quaint and alien: for in the *Iliad* and the *Odyssey* men are praised for the possession of qualities and attributes that we now regard as native gifts for which a man deserves no moral credit. Achilles is praised for swiftness of foot, and Menelaus for having a loud clear voice that can be heard above the noise of battle. Hampshire was forgetting that not long before he made this remark Dr Roger Bannister had been widely praised for the swiftness of foot that had given him the honour of being the first man to run a mile in less than four minutes. It would be no answer to say that praise for Bannister's achievement was directed to the effort and determination that he had put into his training, for if Hampshire or I, after even greater efforts, ran a mile in five minutes, we should neither deserve nor receive the amount or kind of praise that was given to Bannister. The praise was not proportioned to the amount of effort his achievement had cost him: there was praise for his native gift as well as for the use that he had made of it.

Hampshire was overlooking the point that not all praise, and not even all moral praise, is of that kind of which the opposite is moral blame. We may praise a man's intelligence or a woman's beauty, even though these gifts are not the results of choice or effort on the part of those who are endowed with them. A man cannot by taking thought add a cubit to his intellectual stature, but praise for intelligence is both natural and appropriate. It is true that a man cannot reasonably be *blamed* for being by nature ugly or stupid, but to call him handsome or clever is to praise or compliment him, and to remark on his stupidity or ugliness is to dispraise or disparage him.

There are moral qualities as well as intellectual and physical qualities that are rightly praised and prized in spite of not being voluntary and therefore not deserving the kind of moral praise that belongs to effort and choice and action. But these qualities – good nature, a kindly disposition, natural courage or forcefulness of character – are hidden from the view of a moral philosophy that stresses action and conation, and the imperative, emotive and rhetorical functions of moral appraisals, at the cost of obscuring the scope that morality provides for perception, insight and the contemplative understanding, for a species of reflection that is more like aesthetic reflection and contemplation than it is like the other modes of moral reflection. Even Hume, forerunner in this as in so many ways of the fashionable philosophy of today, noticed that we praise talents and gifts as well as moral virtues and achievements (*Enquiries*, §261).

Professor Donald MacKinnon, in *A Study in Ethical Theory*, has given us a timely reminder that we cannot do justice to the complexities of morality if we confine ourselves either to an act-and-consequence ethics or to a character-and-motive ethics. Aristotle and Butler properly emphasize those aspects of morality which have in recent years been overlooked or undervalued when they lay stress on the importance for moral philosophy of the concept of human nature.

But even when we have put off the blinkers of contemporary moral philosophy, and see the width and breadth of morality in all its fullness and variety, we still cannot identify philosophy of life with philosophical morality. There are further questions, questions of such wide scope that it is hard to speak otherwise than vaguely about them, that fall under the heading of philosophy of life. And the chief among them are those questions about the human condition, the human situation, the human predicament, that have come to have such a bad name because it is so hard to speak about them clearly, precisely and with discipline, and so disastrously easy to speak about them vaguely, obscurely and irresponsibly. But what can be done badly can also be done well, and there is scope here too for the pursuit of truth and the diagnosis of falsehood, for the attainment of clarity and the eradication of confusion.

We are in any case inclined to forget how often and how well this kind of thinking continues to be done even in an age of critical and technical philosophy. We can save ourselves from this oversight, and can also find a clue to show where we may look for further progress in this mode of understanding, if we attend to the emphatic reminders given by Arnold and Braithwaite of the role of works of imaginative literature in our thinking about God and man. Poets, dramatists and novelists continue to be as much interested as philosophers have ever been in the riddles and enigmas of human life, and they deal with them more effectively because they present them with concreteness and particularity rather than with the abstractness and indirection that too often mar the attempts of philosophers at this or any task.

Though Arnold and Braithwaite agree that literature is important, they differ characteristically in their accounts of the source and nature of its importance. Braithwaite's subjectivism about morality and religion leads him to be subjectivist about literature, too; to think of literary works as instruments for the expression and propagation of values that are fashioned and not found, created and not discovered. In spite of his own protestations he demeans literature in demeaning religion and morality to a level of arbitrary and unreasoned choice between behaviour policies. Arnold provides a useful corrective. He treats literature as a source and not only as a vehicle of knowledge and understanding. He says of those questions about life and conduct that are for him the essence of religious inquiry that they are properly to be treated by 'literary experience, not reasoning'. But even he fails to allow its full scope and value to this kind of judgement and inquiry, for what he calls 'literary experience', as opposed to reasoning, is itself an important kind of *reasoning*.

Arnold here allows himself to be misled into a false dichotomy that is one of the most common causes and effects of misunderstanding and misrepresentation of religious, moral, critical and literary thought, and of a grossly limited view of the powers of the human understanding in general. The distinction is drawn in many different ways: reason and feeling, reason and imagination, reason and faith, head and heart; but always it involves the same misguided attempt to draw a sharp and clear line between what is and is not within the sphere of reason, truth and knowledge, and the same consequence of excluding from that sphere nearly all that rightly belongs within it. And though this false dichotomy is drawn by many who are uninfluenced by any formal philosophical doctrines, it has the same roots and fruits as the positivistic restriction of meaning and reason to the paradigms of induction and deduction. For it arises from a preoccupation with the formality and generality of mathematics and the sciences and results in the dismissal from the bounds of the concept of reason all that is *informally* subtle and complex.

Even those who avoid the worst extremes of this confusion may show strong signs of its influence. Mr Yvor Winters has insisted as firmly as any philosopher or critic that literature is concerned with truth and knowledge. He defines a poem as 'a statement in words' (*In Defense of Reason*, p. 363), and he counts the appraisal of the truth or falsehood of the statement as a central element in the evaluation of the work of art. But he does not follow through the full consequences of this recognition, and later we find him explaining the difference between a poem and its 'paraphrasable content' by the presence in the one of an emotion or feeling that is absent from the other. Keats' equation of truth with beauty, of beauty with truth, is a cryptic, aphoristic expression of a more thoroughgoing attachment to Winters' initial insight, and so is Ezra Pound's remark that 'the arts, literature, poesy, are a science just as chemistry is a science' (*Literary Essays*, p. 42).

The objections that lead Winters to swerve from the right path are important and persuasive enough to need a fuller and better answer than he gives them. It is possible to give an adequate answer which has the further advantage of explaining how both Winters and his opponents have been misled.

When somebody says that a work of literature embodies thought and knowledge, and that understanding and insight can be derived from it, it is natural to ask 'What do we learn from *Hamlet* or *King Lear* or *War and Peace*?' and to suppose that a statement of what Winters calls the 'paraphrasable content' is a necessary and sufficient means of answering such a question. When it turns out, as it will and must, that the paraphrase manifestly falls short of conveying what we feel to be conveyed by the work itself, and that in any case the paraphrase is usually such a pastiche of platitudes as to contain nothing that any grown-up person could possibly need to *learn*, it is easy to conclude that the thought-content of a play or poem cannot be at all closely connected with what makes us value the work and with the function that it fulfils in our lives. The thought-feeling dichotomy may then seem to provide an answer to the puzzle. We may conclude that the special character of an imaginative work of literature lies not in its content but in the feelings with which it invests what may be merely trite when detached from its imaginative setting.

This view of the matter is doubly mistaken, but it also contains within itself a clue to the correction of one of its mistakes and to an important connection between the nature of philosophy of life and the nature of philosophy more generally. Wittgenstein spoke of philosophy as the activity of assembling *reminders* for a particular purpose, of striving after a clear view of what is already familiar to us but is nevertheless obscured from us by the knots that we tie in our understanding. Wisdom has said that in philosophy we do not acquire knowledge of new facts, but do acquire new knowledge of facts. One of the reasons why it is appropriate to speak both of metaphysics and of reflection on the problems of life as being branches or species of *philosophy* is that they are connected by this concern with gaining or regaining insight into what is overlooked in spite of or because of its extreme familiarity.

It follows that a literary work may contribute to new

knowledge and a new and deeper understanding even when, as often, it does not convey any new information or new facts. In literature, as in the other media in which philosophy of life may be conducted, we often learn without learning anything new. This ceases to appear paradoxical when we attend to the distinction between knowing and *really* knowing, between knowing and fully realizing; and this is a distinction that can be illustrated from many contexts outside even the wide scope of literature and philosophy. What is it like to be a coal miner? What was it like to fight in the trenches in 1914? What does it feel like to orbit the earth in a satellite, to be shipwrecked, to be an orphan, a deaf-mute, or a prisoner of war? We may well know the answers to these questions well enough to describe the relevant experiences in words very like those that would be used by people who, unlike ourselves, have actually had these experiences. And yet it is clear that we might have much to learn of the nature of one of these experience from actually having the experience, even if we were not then able to find words for the description of the experience that were not available to us before it was our own first-hand experience. In such a situation people speak of knowing or realizing for the first time what it *means* to be poor or hungry or hunted.

Somebody who sees the Parthenon or the Rocky Mountains for the first time may similarly find that he has nothing to say about them that has not been said to him a hundred times before, even if he also finds that he now sees much that he had not seen when those words were said to him.

But there is another way of finding out what it meant to be cold and hungry and afraid in the trenches of the Western Front, one which does not involve spending any time in those trenches: and that is to read *Good-bye to All That* by Robert Graves, or some of the writings of Wilfred Owen or Siegfried Sassoon. And in reading a work of literature, as in having a new experience, we may acquire a degree of new knowledge and new understanding that is disproportionate to the number and importance of the new facts that we learn. Some works of literature teach us that which we ourselves do know, but teach us none the less something that we still have need to learn.

But other works or even the same works may teach us something new, and to see this is to be in a position to correct the second mistake in the familiar objection. So far we have concentrated on the sense in which the content of a literary work may be something that we need to learn even if it is something that in another sense we already know. But to treat a 'prose paraphrase' as a statement of the content of a complex imaginative work is to conceal the extent to which such a paraphrase fails in its supposed purpose. Such a summary is detached not only from the form but also from most of the content of the work whose kernel it is meant to convey. What is said by *King Lear* or *War and Peace* is said through the individuality and particularity of the characters, situations and conversations of which the works consist. Above all, it is expressed in different *language* from any that can be used in a short summary or in any paraphrase, and differences of language amount to differences of *meaning* – that is to say, to differences of content.

A small-scale example is sufficient to show the importance of this last point. Winters quotes from Browning's *Serenade at the Villa*:

> So wore night; the East was gray,
>   White the broad-faced hemlock flowers.

He goes on to make some remarks about the language of the passage:

> The verb *wore* means literally that the night passed, but it carries with it connotations of exhaustion and attrition which belong to the condition of the protagonist; and grayness is a colour which we associate with such a condition. If we change the phrase to read: 'Thus night passed', we shall have the same rational meaning, and a meter quite as respectable, but no trace of the power of the line: the connotation of *wore* will be lost, and the connotation of *gray* will remain merely in a state of ineffective potentiality.
>
> *In Defense of Reason*, pp. 365–6

In spite of using the word 'connotations' in a way that involves him in contradicting his own main point, Winters here represents a difference of *meaning* as if it were a difference only in the emotion with which one and the same ('rational') meaning is invested. The word 'passed' certainly could not function in a paraphrase as a means of conveying exactly what the word 'wore' conveys in the poem, but that is because it means something different.

These points taken together indicate a degree of overlapping in scope and function between literature and religion that sets in a new light the idea of the Bible 'Designed to be Read as Literature'. Braithwaite and Arnold, and perhaps also Tillich and the Bishop of Woolwich, think of the Bible in this way; not indeed as something to be read for entertainment or 'for aesthetic reasons' but as fulfilling a function that belongs to other literature as well as to the Bible, the function of throwing light for us on aspects of our lives with which we are already familiar but not deeply enough familiar; of which we have some grasp, but not an adequate grasp. In the same light we can see also how natural it is that others should have been tempted to reverse the equation and offer us a literature designed to be read as the Bible.

There are lessons on this point to be drawn from precedents in ancient Greece. They are usefully expounded by Professor E. A. Havelock in his *Preface to Plato*. He reminds us that in classical Greece literature was conceived of as a medium of instruction, as designed to increase not only understanding, but also knowledge and skill, including even knowledge of practical and technical subjects, such as agriculture, strategy and astronomy, as well as a general knowledge of history and geography and human nature and experience. Poetry provided 'a massive repository of useful knowledge, a sort of encyclopedia of ethics, politics, history and technology which the effective citizen was required to learn as the core of his educational equipment. Poetry represented not something we call by that name, but an indoctrination which today would be comprised in a shelf of text-books and works of reference' (p. 27).

Plato's notorious hostility to poets and playwrights arose from his recognition that they were influential in forming ideas on subjects which in his view ought to be the preserves of specialized experts. Plato's attack on Homer and the tragedians is not to be seen as a side-issue, but is at the centre of his revolutionary programme for educational and political reform. He wished to set not only moral inquiry, but all inquiry in general, on the sure path of a science, and he therefore felt bound to attack the pretensions of literature and its exponents and expositors to inculcate political and moral understanding, strategical and rhetorical skill, or any other sound learning.

Havelock explains the close connection between Plato's critique of imaginative literature and his metaphysics and theory of knowledge. Plato was suspicious of literature not only because he believed that its authors had all been mistaken in their conclusions on the questions they purported to answer, but because in his view the answering of any questions calls for a formality and generality of method that necessarily could not be followed in a work of the mere imagination, one that dealt in the concrete, particular and individual instead of the abstract universals of the Theory of Forms. What Havelock does not sufficiently stress, if he recognizes it at all, is the extent to which literature in our own day, as well as in the time of Homer or Plato, continues to fulfil its function of teaching us or reminding us what life is like.

The art of the sermon is a literary art, one of the junctions where literature and religion meet; and preaching, like litera- ture and philosophy, largely consists in 'the assembling of reminders for a particular purpose'. How often does one hear anything said in a sermon that one has never heard before? How often does one hear anything said in a sermon that one has not heard said *in a sermon* before? But many sermons are good sermons, even though few of them arrive at surprising results. A sermon may help a congregation as the prophet Nathan helped David when he brought him to a full and vivid realization of what he had only latently and inadequately recognized.

A good work of imaginative literature, like a good sermon, proceeds by the method of concrete, particular cases, the method that Aristotle commended when he spoke of poetry as more serious and more philosophical than history. Aristotle's remark is a corrective to Plato and to any thinker who sup- poses that there cannot be thought unless there is the generality and system of mathematical thought. When we think about life and conduct, just as when we think about knowledge and its grounds, we must engage in that exploration of the similarities and differences between particulars and particulars on which even the more formal and systematic modes of thought are in the end dependent. In Ezra Pound's words, 'Art does not avoid universals, it strikes at them all the harder in that it strikes through particulars' (*Literary Essays*, p. 420). The literary power of accurate and precise portrayal of complexity, individuality, particularity, is as much as any human power a power of human thought. Literature is one of the functions of the human reason. We must not follow Sartre in his conclusion that the rich complexity and particularity of moral considerations is an obstacle to rational thought about moral choice, or Hare in his insistence that the evident rationality of moral inquiry fits it for a hypothetico-deductive mould.

There are discoveries and discoveries and discoveries. Strether's growing awareness outstrips the scope of the new facts that come to his notice. It was not new information that prompted Housman to speak, when he heard the church bells from the tower, of finding that on his tongue the taste was sour of all he ever did; but what these words record is a realization and a recognition, an opening of eyes that were already open but which had not seen what they had seen. Harold Pinter presents in *The Caretaker* a man who believes and tediously repeats that he is on his way to Sidcup, but who never takes any of the steps that would bring him nearer to Sidcup. Through one instance of a man's failure to understand himself and his own intentions, Pinter presents a thousand instances of failure in self-knowledge.

In tragedy there is often recognition even when there is no formal ἀναγνώρισις. The story of Oedipus is the story of the discovery of material facts – a birth, a marriage, and a death – but also and supremely the story of the discovery and recognition of a man's whole situation and of man's whole situation: a story of growth in knowledge and self-knowledge. Here as often in life and literature the tragic ἁμαρτία is a failure of vision as much as or more than a failure of will. And this helps us to see why Socrates held that there are not here two kinds of failure but one; that no man does wrong willingly, wittingly, consciously; that every failure in action is or is a consequence of a failure in understanding; that complete knowledge and complete self-knowledge would make us powerless to do the wrongs that we do and suffer.

When Hamlet tried and succeeded in his plan to 'catch the conscience of the King' it was not by telling the King anything that the King did not already know: it was by changing the nature and quality of his knowledge, by bringing into the strong light of day what was there in the cloudier regions of the King's own mind. William Golding's *Lord of the Flies* may not be news to anybody with any experience of children and of human beings in general, but those to whom it is not news may still learn something from it about children and other human beings.

Moral discoveries often include discoveries of particular material facts, but the cases that are most liable to be mis-described are those where no new facts are learned, or where the scope and value of the discovery are disproportionate to the importance of the new facts. One may have all 'the facts' and still have much to learn from thinking them through. There is a kind of useful advice, and perhaps the only kind of useful advice, by which one person helps another to think through and to connect rightly with other facts and other circumstances a set of facts and circumstances which are all already well known to both of them. Some phases of some moral reflections, some instances of moral or prudential advice, consist in part in trying to foresee the causal consequences of this or that course of action. But another and equally important element in deliberating or advising consists in reflecting on the intrinsic character, the internal relations and the logical consequences of the various courses of action; in considering what it is that one would be committed to in being committed to this or that judgement or action or decision.

The examples I have given further illustrate the application to morality of Wisdom's remarks about the search for elusive patterns in bewildering masses of detail, remarks which are also applicable to the quest for metaphysical or epistemological understanding. Wittgenstein's metaphor of finding one's way – 'A philosophical problem has the form "I don't know my way about" ' – has the same double relevance to my theme. Both in the perplexities of technical philosophy and in the mazes of practical life we often lose our bearings and need guidance rather than information, a perspective on what we can already see rather than news of what is over the hill or beyond the horizon. The informal complexities of metaphysics and the informal complexities of practical life are structurally similar, and call for similar methods of treatment. This kinship of structure and method is one of the sources of failure to distinguish philosophical morality from the philosophy of morality, but it is also the basis for the sound observation that lies behind the mistake: that morality and metaphysics, though mutually independent, are not mutually irrelevant.

The proverbs in which popular and conventional wisdom is expressed clearly illustrate the logic of the method that belongs both to technical philosophy and to philosophy of life. A proverb, like a philosophical thesis, is usually either a platitude or a paradox. It seldom or never tells anybody anything that is both new and straightforwardly true. But by citing the platitude that a stitch in time saves nine, or the paradox that tomorrow never comes, one man may valuably remind another of something that he knows but has not remembered when it would most help him to see the case that is before him now, to place it in its relation to other cases that call for a similar judgement and that he knows how to judge. Proverbial generalizations fall under Mill's generalization about generalizations, in that they serve as *memoranda* whereby we may compendiously bring to bear on a puzzling or disputed case the relevant cases that no longer puzzle us (*A System of Logic*, Book II, Chapter III, § 4).

By the same light we can see why the fact that one proverb contradicts another need not impair the functioning of either. Many hands make light work, but too many cooks spoil the broth. Look before you leap, but he who hesitates is lost. By using one of these proverbs on one occasion, I do not bar myself from using the other on another occasion. The two occasions may differ in just the ways that make them call for two different reminders. Rashness and indecisiveness both occur often enough to provide work for both the proverbs.

These reflections also help us to understand what is right and what is wrong with the platitude that moral progress lags behind technical and scientific progress. For there are differences in kind between moral and technical progress that make it misleading to try to compare them on the same scale. Socrates and Wilberforce achieved moral progress, just as surely as Archimedes or Newton or Einstein achieved scientific progress. But the general differences between science and morality involve differences in the application of the concept of progress to the two modes of inquiry.

Some of these differences come to light if we ask why nobody complains that literary progress or architectural progress lags behind technical progress. Have we advanced in literature since the time of Homer, or in architecture since the building of the Parthenon? An achievement in moral or philosophical progress continues to be of contemporary interest and importance in something like the sense in which a classic work of art retains its primary function from age to age, while the classics of mathematics or science survive only as objects of antiquarian interest. Morality and philosophy differ both from literature and the fine arts, in which it might be said (misleadingly but pointfully) that there is nothing identifiable as progress, and from science and mathematics, in which there is a more or less precisely traceable line of progress. That they are linked with literature and the arts, and that their kind of progress is different from that of science and mathematics, makes it a natural mistake, though still a mistake, to say that they do not allow of progress at all, or that progress in them, though possible, does not in fact occur.

As soon as Euclid has written the letters Q.E.D., or Newton has completed the *Principia*, or Einstein has published the epoch-making paper, the epoch is made, and progress has been achieved that may be credited at once to the whole of mankind. Once they have made their moves, those moves have been definitively made, and while others will teach them and learn them, nobody else will have to *make* those moves again. Progress in morality is not like that, but it is progress none the less. In morality the progress, the discovery, has to be made again and again, by each individual in and for himself. Einstein would still have made progress in physics even if there had never been more than two or three people who understood what progress he had made. One might also say that Socrates and St Francis and Wilberforce have made moral progress on behalf of mankind, even if nobody is ever convinced by what they say, but these cases are importantly different. There is a dimension to moral progress that is not found in scientific and mathematical progress. One who comes after Socrates or St Francis or Wilberforce both can make and ought to make the same step forward for himself. Moral discoveries are discoveries for each new generation and each new individual:

they cannot be accepted from a tradition or on authority as many other discoveries can.

Proverbial wisdom again provides a useful illustration. It is so well known as to be a proverb and a platitude that *si jeunesse savait, si vieillesse pouvait* much of human life would be better ordered. But the full recognition and realization of the truth of the platitude is laboriously achieved by every man for himself. Even when the form of expression is novel, the content will often be familiar, and the value of 'what oft was thought, but ne'er so well expressed' may lie not only in the elegance of the expression but also in its effectiveness at conveying what is known well but not well enough. When we read the Maxims of La Rochefoucauld we may be entitled to say 'How true!' and yet not entitled to say, dismissively, that we knew it all before.

The relevance of these points to the questions raised at the beginning of this lecture may now be made plainer. Recent epistemology or metaphysics has at least this relevance to philosophy of life, that it is part of the function of a complete epistemology to reveal the nature and to display the objectivity of philosophy of life, and also to describe the sources of the current misconceptions of its nature and challenges to its objectivity. But there is a second and at least equally important way in which recent philosophy is relevant to philosophy of life. In acquiring a new understanding of the nature and mode of operation of metaphysical philosophy we have learned to recognize the profound similarities of technique between metaphysical philosophy itself and philosophical reflection on some questions that are not questions of pure philosophy, including questions that belong to the philosophy of life. Since the techniques of pure philosophy are substantially those of literature and of the other media, including theology, in which the philosophy of life and philosophical morality are most fitly conducted, it is to be expected that those who have a good grasp of the skills of pure philosophy should also have the capacity, even if they may lack the will, to make contributions to philosophy of life and philosophical morality. I am not suggesting that this kind of philosophical work can or should be conducted only by philosophers, even though it may still be called philosophical when it is done by poets, playwrights or preachers;

but I am suggesting that there is no good reason why those who have learned a technique in the course of their practice of metaphysical philosophy should not apply that technique to questions that call for philosophical treatment but are not questions of metaphysical philosophy.

Contemporary professional philosophers have understandably hesitated to attempt this task. They are more intensely conscious than their predecessors were of being *professional* philosophers, and they are aware that their main function as professional specialists is to inquire into the technical questions of philosophy, the questions of pure philosophy or metaphysics. Their disinclination to consider the questions of applied philosophy leaves a vacuum to be filled by amateurs, most of whom are amateurs in the bad sense of the word, turning away from the vices of professionalism so firmly that they do not see or practise any of its virtues. The Sunday reviewers will continue to welcome the inanities and pomposities of a succession of pretentious minor prophets at least until the same kind of work is attempted by those who are better qualified to do it.

A second and more regrettable reason why professional philosophers neglect this kind of work is that many of them doubt its rationality and objectivity. When they express these doubts they are making mistakes within their own proper professional field of metaphysical philosophy. They are making the mistake of concluding that what is an informal mode of reasoning cannot be a mode of reasoning at all, the mistake of underestimating the internal variety of the concepts of reason and truth.

I have already given arguments and instances to show that these mistakes are mistakes. The case against them can be strengthened by referring to some examples within the work of contemporary philosophers themselves, which show that some points of pure epistemology have valuable application to questions that fall outside the range of technical philosophy; that to some mistakes in applied philosophy there are exactly analogous mistakes in pure philosophy that have been diagnosed and corrected by professional philosophers working within their own professional compass.

Misunderstandings about universals and generality, and related confusions about the efficacy of informal reasoning by the presentation of particular actual or imaginary cases, are perhaps the commonest philosophical obstacles to the proper conduct of moral and political thought. In Wisdom's article on Existentialism, to which I have referred earlier, we find a diagnosis of some widespread muddles about happiness and the *summum bonum* whose exposure and treatment call for close attention to 'the idea that the meaning of a word is an object' and the idea that to characterize happiness (or justice or tragedy or juvenile delinquency or democracy or religion) is to isolate and describe some element or ingredient that is common and peculiar to all the instances falling under the general term in question.

Judges in courts of law sometimes, like philosophical sceptics, impugn the rationality and objectivity of procedures of reasoning that they themselves can operate with admirable rationality and objectivity. They often say, when hearing and assessing claims for damages, that it is impossible to set a financial value on a lost limb, a lost life or lost happiness. But they show in summing up or giving judgement that they know better than they say they know. The mistake in their theory, which fortunately has little effect on their practice, is a philosophical mistake, a special case of one that is often made and often corrected by pure epistemologists. Because there is evidently no precise sum that is *the* correct sum of damages on this occasion, they are led to say, though not to believe, that there are no rights and wrongs about the matter at all. They show by their practice how well they know that it may be obvious in a particular case that five shillings is too little, and a million pounds is too much, to represent the appropriate sum of damages. And if we can know of one particular sum that it is too little, and of another particular sum that it is too much, we have already embarked on the rational, case-by-case procedure of determining the right amount. Neither here nor anywhere else do difficulties about vagueness, complexity and borderlines amount to good or even relevant grounds for a despairing scepticism.

There are other cases where philosophical confusions and their close kindred do positive practical harm. It is often said that poverty or prejudice or superstition or ignorance or error will never be wholly eradicated, and it is too often supposed that it is therefore useless to persist in our efforts to eradicate error, ignorance, superstition, prejudice or poverty. But the argument is dangerously muddled even if the premise is true, and the muddle is a typically philosophical muddle. From the fact that there will always be pain and disease, if it is a fact, it does not follow that it is pointless to try to cure this particular disease or to palliate this particular pain.

Important as some of them are, these are all relatively small-scale examples, calling for the piecemeal or tactical application of philosophical acuteness or experience. Philosophy of life has traditionally been conducted also and mainly on a larger terrain and with a more comprehensive, strategic objective. It remains to be seen whether we still have need and scope, men and resources, for these larger operations.

In a letter to Norman Malcolm, quoted on pages 39–40 of Malcolm's *Memoir*, Wittgenstein wrote: 'What is the use of studying philosophy if all that it does for you is to enable you to talk with some plausibility about some abstract questions of logic, etc., and if it does not improve your thinking about the important question of everyday life? . . .' In this and other letters and other writings Wittgenstein does something to explain how he thinks that such thinking can be conducted: on page 43 he is quoted as saying that Tolstoy's philosophy 'is most true when it's *latent* in the story'. We have seen for ourselves that Wittgenstein is right in thinking that it is possible and important to look to works of imaginative literature for such 'philosophy'. We still need to see whether there is any place, and if so what place there is, for philosophical thinking about life to be conducted in explicitly philosophical dress, and whether our consideration of literature and morality and theology can help us to answer these contentious questions.

8 · Recollection

Both religion and philosophy have withdrawn in recent centuries from much territory over which they used to claim sovereignty, but where they now recognize the underived and autonomous authority of the natural sciences. The main cause of the withdrawal was an increase in the *de facto* power of mathematics and the sciences in those realms, and its main effect has been a reduction in the area of conflict between physical and biological scientists and proponents of transcendentalist and supernaturalist accounts of the world and life and man. I have suggested that philosophers have withdrawn too far, and have largely abandoned tasks that they could still perform. In particular, there are natural causes but no sufficient reasons why philosophers neglect the problems and questions that belong to the branch of applied philosophy that I have called philosophy of life, and reserve nearly all their energy and ingenuity for the study of epistemology or metaphysics.

Theology, by contrast, has become increasingly preoccupied with its function as the study of how to live. It has so far turned away from its concern with a transcendent world and from its traditional claim to offer a comprehensive and definitive truth that in some of its forms it has ceased to be recognizable as theology, and has become instead the kind of philosophy that professional philosophers neglect. It may continue to use God's name, but only in complete detachment from his nature.

A sharp division of labour has been effected. Plato and Aristotle, Hobbes and Spinoza, Kant and Hegel all contributed both to technical philosophy, to epistemology and metaphysics, and to the search for answers to the problems of life and conduct. In recent times these tasks have been seen as two separate specialisms. Philosophers abjure preaching and moral teaching; philosophers of life, in the guise of theologians – or novelists, poets, playwrights – take no interest, or only a superficial and ll-informed interest, in the questions of metaphysics and theory of knowledge.

We can grasp this situation better, and can see more clearly the good reasons why these two activities were once combined and the good reasons why they have now become separated, if we look back to some of the classic metaphysical and moral philosophers of the past. We need to know how they conceived the connection between what we now call their two distinct functions, and also whether we have been led by our more recent predecessors to exaggerate the distinction between them.

The so-called 'revolution in philosophy' in the twentieth century has been an empiricist, anti-transcendentalist movement. Its initial attack was directed against the Hegelian idealist philosophers of the immediately preceding generation. But like all revolutionary movements, it was prompted by iconoclastic fervour to turn its guns on wider targets. What was at first a metaphysical critique of a particular set of metaphysical doctrines grew into a self-defeating rejection of metaphysics in general and as such. An extremist minority went so far as to give the impression that nothing of any importance or signficance had been achieved in philosophy before the date of the revolution itself. A specific revolt against a specific tradition led in the end to a wholesale rejection of all that was traditional.

There are two effects of this undiscriminating zeal that are of particular relevance here. (1) In their hostility towards the metaphysicians of the past the innovators failed to distinguish between the metaphysical content of traditional philosophical doctrines and the idioms in which that content had been expressed, and they therefore did not see how much of earlier philosophy was a contribution to the progress of the very enterprise in which they themselves, though using a different idiom, were still engaged. (2) They were also misled into such a wholesale rejection of classical metaphysics that they peremptorily proscribed the activity of moral teaching which the classical philosophers had combined with their metaphysical theorizing, and did not recognize that this was a sufficiently separate activity to need separate treatment.

Nothing in the characteristic principles and procedures of recent philosophy requires or supports this hostility towards traditional philosophy. On the contrary, it can be shown by the use of those procedures and principles themselves that contemporary epistemologists and even the most uncompromisingly transcendentalist metaphysicians of the past are contributors to a common enterprise. Positivists and their fellow-travellers have here committed exactly the mistake that they have so often exposed when it has been committed by other philosophers and on other topics: the mistake of failing to distinguish linguistic forms of expression from the logical content that is expressed by them, the outward forms of words from the uses to which they have been put.

We have seen in comparing and contrasting Homeric theology with other and later uses of its characteristic formulae that an unchanging form of words may be used for radically different purposes, and may even on one occasion express something incompatible with what it expresses on another. It is therefore a mistake to suppose that two people who use the same form of words must be saying the same thing in any stronger sense. Similarly, two people may use radically different forms of words, so different that they appear to be contradicting each other, while nevertheless they are making the same point.

This distinction between outward form and logical structure may be illustrated by an analogy from outside philosophy. When we play chess we usually use a board and wooden or ivory pieces, which are literally and physically moved to represent the moves in the game. But it is theoretically possible, and for some gifted players practically possible, to play 'mental chess', to play chess in their heads without any material pieces at all. Chess has sometimes been played with live human beings as pieces. There is no theoretical reason why it should not be played with real live kings, queens, knights and bishops.

These are three very different ways of playing chess, but they are all ways of playing *chess*: they are not three different games, but three different ways of playing the same game, three different notations in which the moves may be expressed and recorded. It could well happen that three pairs of people who were playing according to the three different conventions made the same moves at every stage, so that the records of the games in a written chess notation were identical. And it could not happen that a queen sacrifice or an exchange of bishops was a wise

move in one of the games and a foolish move in another, considered simply as a chess move. The choice of notation could
affect the moves only in ways that were irrelevant to the game
as a game of chess. It is said that one master, playing in an
exhibition game, became so attached to the waitress who played
the white queen that he declined an opportunity to make an
advantageous exchange of queens. One might imagine a game
played by oriental potentates with prisoners of war according
to a convention whereby every captured piece is dispatched to
and by the Lord High Executioner. But all this is irrelevant to
the game of chess.

It would be possible for one of the oriental potentates to
play chess by correspondence or by telephone with a western
mathematician who played in his head: and neither would need
to know what pieces, if any, the other was using.

I suggest that we can find here a close analogy for the
relation between traditional metaphysical philosophy and contemporary epistemological philosophy, and in general for the
unity of philosophical inquiry that underlies the plurality and
diversity of the idioms in which it has been and is conducted.
Metaphysics has been variously conceived and expressed as a
study of the most general features of the world and experience,
as the exploration of a transcendent world of immaterial forms
or universals, as the natural history of man and his understanding, as a logical study of concepts, or as a linguistic examination
of the uses or usages of words. There is room for philosophical
debate about and between these rival conceptions and their
rival idioms; for controversy in the metaphysics of metaphysics
about which if any of these idioms is the native language of the
metaphysician. But this controversy is as irrelevant to the
structure and outcome of inquiry and debate *within* metaphysics as the choice of chessmen is to the course and conclusion
of a game of chess. In both cases it is only by confusion or by the
intrusion of some extraneous motive that a player will allow the
nature of his idiom to govern his choice of moves.

A reading list for an undergraduate essay on our knowledge
of the external world may include Locke and Berkeley and
Moore and McTaggart and Ayer and Austin: and in spite of
the great range of metaphilosophical views represented by these
six philosophers, and the corresponding diversity of costume in

which they clothe their thoughts on the philosophy of perception, the pupil will recognize that all six are dealing with the same problems, and that their arguments and conclusions can confirm or contradict each other across the idioms. They are all playing the same game with different counters.

If a man insists on discussing Freedom (with a capital F) or the *concept* or the *logic* of freedom, or the use of the *word* 'freedom', it is usually best to allow him the choice of weapons. To propose and defend a different choice of idiom would be to change the subject from the philosophy of freedom to the philosophy of philosophy.

Russell's problem of universals is Plato's problem of the one and the many, and his solution in *The Problems of Philosophy* is Plato's solution translated into a different language. Russell's problem of negation in *Human Knowledge* is Plato's problem of 'not-being' in the *Sophist*, and they produce the same solution in spite of the differences between a logical and an ontological dress.

The contemporary epistemologist can make use, ought to make use, and does make use of the epistemological work of his predecessors, regardless of the idioms in which they executed it, and regardless therefore of their conceptions, which may differ from his own, of the nature of epistemological inquiry.

To recognize that the ontological theories of traditional metaphysicians are offered as solutions of epistemological problems that are still discussed in other idioms is to preserve a respect for our philosophical predecessors that has sometimes been lacking among some of our contemporaries. It is to see that philosophy is a continuing conversation, and not an activity that began or ended in 1900. But the recognition brings a new danger of its own. Even when an understanding of what Professor Wisdom has called 'The Metamorphosis of Metaphysics' cures us of the philistinism of dismissing all traditional philosophy as antique *bric-à-brac*, we may not carry the work of reclamation far enough. We may think that because one large part of what the ancient and modern classical philosophers did has now been taken over by the natural sciences, and another large part has been continued by professional, technical, epistemological philosophers, there is therefore nothing left of what the old philosophers did that calls for further philosophical attention.

This is a natural mistake, but still a mistake. Plato and Spinoza and Hobbes and Hegel were certainly engaged in pure philosophy to an extent that may easily be hidden from us by the idioms in which they conducted it. But they were also concerned to fulfil other and non-epistemological functions, and they were engaged in them *as philosophers*. The very theories of theirs to which we may now look for guidance on the problems of pure philosophy were also designed to make a contribution to what I have called applied philosophy. In particular, they contributed and meant to contribute to the philosophy of life, an enterprise that they rightly understood to include but also to transcend philosophical morality. Philosophy of life is also undertaken by many who are not philosophers: poets, playwrights, novelists, religious and moral teachers. That may help to explain why many philosophers no longer regard it as part of their business, but it does not justify them in treating it as an illegitimate or philosophically disreputable enterprise.

There are a number of separate types of inquiry which, though distinct from metaphysics or pure philosophy, call for the attention of trained and skilled philosophers because they directly involve the use of the *techniques* of pure philosophy. The first and most straightforward is one that in practice is not often distinguished from pure philosophy, though it is logically quite distinct from it – namely, the process of removing the philosophical perplexities of particular individuals or groups of people.

This process has sometimes been called 'therapeutic philosophy', and it is what Wisdom and others have had in mind when they have spoken of parallels between philosophy and psychoanalysis. It shades into, or forms part of, the process of *teaching* philosophy. To distinguish such a use of philosophical techniques from the activity of pure philosophy itself is to draw a very fine but nevertheless important distinction of purpose or objective which has been hidden by the identity of technique. The fine distinction is important because it is by overlooking it that some philosophers have been led to deny that philosophy can be practically useful and others have been led to deny that there is such a thing as *pure* philosophy.

The issues here are closely parallel to those I discussed in the first lecture when I spoke of pure and applied philosophy by analogy with pure and applied mathematics, and these same distinctions will be useful to us here again.

I suggested that the pure philosopher or mathematician sets out to answer a pure *a priori* question solely for the sake of answering that pure *a priori* question, but that it is often necessary and possible to study such a question for the sake of some end beyond the pure study of the question itself. The most familiar cases are those where the answering of mathematical questions is of value to the purposes of the physicist, economist or engineer. I now suggest, by analogy, that a philosopher whose aim is to relieve the anxiety or to resolve the perplexity of one who is worried or puzzled by a philosophical question, is applying the techniques of pure philosophy to the achievement of an objective that does not belong to pure philosophy.

This distinction is so fine as to be almost academic, but it points towards another that is of greater scope and consequence. Somebody who uses one of the forms of words whose primary use is to ask a question of pure philosophy (Can we, or do we, or how can we know that other people have feelings, that the sun will rise tomorrow, that this action was free and that one done under compulsion?) may be concerned with the pure principles of epistemology partly or only because they can throw light on actual facts and situations. Every philosophical scepticism has as its shadow, and as one of its main psychological sources (as opposed to logical or metaphysical grounds) a *genuine* doubt about whether we can and do know this or that proposition, or any proposition of this or that kind, to be true. Every philosophical or metaphysical scepticism has as its twin a genuine caution that belongs not to pure philosophy but to the life of man outside philosophy. There is to every philosophical scepticism, as what might be called its 'contingent copy', a genuine doubt about whether we can *as a matter of fact* have knowledge, or knowledge of this or that particular kind.

The kinship or twinship between these two kinds of scepticism is shown clearly by the forms in which the arguments and counter-arguments of metaphysical sceptics and their opponents are usually clothed, and which often serve to disguise a metaphysical scepticism, making it look as if it were the empirical caution in whose costume it is dressed. The sceptic of the senses reminds us of the *fact* of illusion, of the actual occurrence of occasions on which what was taken to be an oasis turned out to be a mirage. The sceptic about other minds refers to villains who have smiled and smiled, the moral sceptic to those whose misplaced moral confidence has led to tyranny and inquisition.

In each of these cases – and there are analogous instances for all the other scepticisms and the kinds of knowledge they impugn – all that a metaphysical sceptic needs or can make use of is the logical possibility of illusion and mistake: the fact of its occurrence is irrelevant to his thesis and its grounds. Both he and his opponents (such as Moore) often disguise by their 'material' modes of expression and by their choice of actual examples their underlying concern with abstract *a priori* issues. But not all those who use this idiom are on all occasions concerned with the problems of pure philosophy for their own sake. The ontological idiom would not be a natural guise for purely epistemological inquiry unless there were other forms of inquiry, closely related to the epistemological, for which it is the normal dress. We need to recognize more clearly than most recent philosophers have been prepared to recognize the extent to which philosophical techniques and distinctions may be used and are used in the pursuit of objectives distinct from those of pure philosophy. In many instances what may look like a disguised epistemological perplexity is in fact a contingent copy clothed in its own appropriate costume. For every problem in the standard corpus of technical metaphysical problems there is an analogue that lies outside the limits of metaphysics, but to which reflection on the metaphysical problem is decisively relevant.

At the end of his paper 'The Concept of Mind' Wisdom underlines the logical distinctness of the question that is at issue between himself and the sceptic from any issue of fact about our knowledge of others:

When we claim that someone knows the thoughts and feelings of another we do not deny any of those facts about what ultimately gives a right to make statements about thoughts and feelings to which the Sceptic draws our attention. And therefore what the Sceptic says does not show that what we claim could not be true nor that what we claim is false.

This does not show that what we claim is true; it does not

settle the question whether sometimes we do know what is in the mind of another. This is a question of fact and not of philosophy. But the fact is we do.

Other Minds, Second Edition, p. 244

Wisdom is right in thinking that what lies behind the disguise of the ontological or factual idiom, and the reference to actual instances of illusion, may be a pure *a priori* concern with epistemological questions, and in my remarks on the unity of epistemology and the diversity of its idioms I have made full allowance for the possibility and frequency of this phenomenon. But there are cases where there is an additional concern with the facts, one that is not a mere appearance arising from a misleading choice of idioms, and there are many cases where the concern with the facts is the primary or even exclusive concern, where the apparent epistemological motive is itself the disguise for what would on other occasions be its 'contingent copy' – namely, the expression of real doubt or caution about our everyday knowledge of things and persons.

A further reference to Wisdom's example of the accountant and the lawyer will make this distinction clearer. A pupil in accountancy may in the course of writing an examination paper calculate the answer to the question 'Would a firm with these assets and these liabilities be solvent?' It may be that the given assets and liabilities are exactly those met with by the examiner in an actual case in his practical experience, a case in which he was concerned with the question of fact 'Is this firm solvent?' In spite of the structural identity of the examples, and of the calculations they call for, the examination candidate is answering a pure *a priori* question, and not a question of fact. He traces out the same logical or mathematical connections as the practising accountant, but he is answering a different question, one about the pure principles that are applied by the practical accountant. A law student may similarly consider whether on the facts of a certain hypothetical case the conduct of the defendant amounts to negligence, and may later meet an actual case whose facts conform to those of the hypothetical case.

The parallel with the philosophical cases is very close. Somebody whose doubt or difficulty is about whether in fact he or anybody knows a certain proposition to be true, or any proposition of a certain kind to be true, may be in such a position that all that he now needs in order to answer his question of fact is a grasp of certain *a priori* connections. As Wisdom indicates, the fact is that we do know many propositions to be true within every one of the kinds that have been subject to sceptical doubt, but a misunderstanding of the logical character of any one of those kinds may lead to a doubt which is itself a doubt about the truth or falsehood of the claim that we *do* know this or that rather than about the epistemological relations that must be examined in the process of answering the doubt. This is comparable with the case in which my doubt is about whether the firm is solvent, though I am in such a position that all I now need to do in order to resolve my doubt is to perform a pure calculation.

In the practice of philosophy there is commonly a confused mixture of the logically distinct elements of 'genuine' doubt and philosophical doubt. Scepticism about induction or the future or the past is reinforced psychologically by a consciousness of the *fact* that it is difficult in many cases to predict the future or to find out about what happened in the past. Philosophical scepticism about other minds is reinforced by the real difficulty we often have in trying to understand each other. Moral perplexity feeds and waters philosophical scepticism about morality. Metaphysical disputes about free will and determinism are fuelled by the practical difficulty of determining in many and important cases whether this or that man is responsible for this or that deed or misdeed. There is scope in all these cases for the application of the pure principles of epistemology, both to separate the distinct elements and to contribute to the resolution of the composite difficulty by answering the epistemological problem that is one of its components.

The indeterminate boundary between technical philosophy and philosophy of life runs parallel with, even if it does not coincide with, the indeterminate boundary between the philosophical questions that 'the plain man' feels to be 'real' problems and those that he thinks of as irremediably academic and unprofitable. Disputes about free will are of interest to many whose philosophical interests are not otherwise well developed, and this is connected with the fact that such disputes, though they are in some forms as purely metaphysical as any others in philosophy, are liable to lead to or to arise from reflections about the theory and practice of reward and punishment and practical perplexities about praise and blame. Sometimes they are also combined, in more or less confused and confusing ways, with speculations about the future growth and results and effects of psychological and social and behavioural sciences, or with conflicts about the pursuit and application of the techniques and discoveries of such sciences.

The proverb *tout comprendre, c'est tout pardonner* is not a proposition of metaphysical philosophy, but it is highly relevant to a full development of the problem of free will. Those who are exercised about the free-will problem, even if they study it and discuss it in a purely logical or epistemological idiom, are often genuinely exercised about whether in private and in public life they can justifiably assign praise and blame, reward and punishment. In asking whether a theoretically complete understanding would or should always prompt them to forgive, they are also asking whether they ought in practice always to forgive even in the absence of such an understanding. Those who defend determinism are often less concerned with the purely philosophical issues for their own sake than with warning us not to jump to conclusions about matters that lie outside technical philosophy: not to jump too soon to moral judgements of ourselves and others, not to forget how much more we know than once we did of the springs of human action and how much more we may hope or fear to learn. There are connections between the classical free-will puzzle and the questions that Socrates answered with his paradox that no man does wrong willingly; and nobody has ever thought that his interest in pure philosophy was his only philosophical interest.

The intertwining of metaphysical and substantive questions is perhaps at its most intimate in moral philosophy and philosophical morality. Some of the lessons that can be learned from well-directed metaphysical study of the nature of moral reasoning are directly helpful in the logically distinct activity of reflection on moral questions themselves. Some of the most serious misapprehensions of the logical character of morality are usually associated with confusions in first-order moral thinking. We saw earlier that a mixture of epistemological motives with the moral motive of opposition to authoritarianism can lead not only to epistemological confusion but also to moral confusion. Nowell-Smith was led astray in his account of the metaphysic of morals by the promptings of his moral consciousness against tyranny and religious persecution. Those who cry that morality is a matter of personal choice usually do so in opposition to what they rightly or wrongly regard as moral dogmatism or misuse of authority. But if all morality were a matter of personal choice then it would be a matter of personal choice whether it is proper to exercise authority in any particular case, or at all. The argument that the exercise of authority is morally repugnant because morality is a matter of personal choice is an incoherent amalgam of bad morality and bad epistemology, and its diagnosis and correction call for better moral thinking as well as for better epistemological thinking.

Controversies about the universality of moral rules and their application to concrete instances may also involve complex inter-connections between epistemology and substantive morality. Sound moral judgement and effective deliberation call for a mistrust of the fixity of conventional moral rules, and of all other moral rules; for open-mindedness, flexibility and adaptability, awareness of the complexities of action, motive and experience. An adequate metaphysical account of the nature of moral reasoning will show how these complexities and individualities can be reconciled with the requirement of consistency that moral reasoning, like all other reasoning, must satisfy. My remarks about Hare and Sartre in an earlier lecture pointed out some of the ill-effects of failure to achieve this reconciliation. To believe that a choice must be made between the imposition of universal unexceptionable rules and the total abandonment of rationality in ethics is to halt between two opinions each of which is both morally and epistemologically misguided. The objectivity of morality is compatible with its 'situational relativity', with the fact that 'circumstances alter cases'. There is no accurate and general way of setting out principles that yield correct judgement on all the cases, and if there were such a set of principles it could only be arrived at by first knowing the answers in all the particular cases; but morality may be objective without being in that sense absolute.

Moral philosophy and free will are philosophical topics

with a direct and explicit bearing on human action and feeling and choice. The metaphysical problem of time has more of the air of a wholly abstract and technical problem, and yet it too is linked with human hopes and fears, and so comes within the scope of applied as well as of pure philosophy. Those who have spoken of the unreality of time – Parmenides, Spinoza, Leibniz, Bradley, McTaggart – have all to some degree, and some to a high degree, been preoccupied with issues that reach beyond the range of pure epistemology. Though the doctrine that time is an illusion, and the arguments by which metaphysicians have defended it, can make a contribution to our understanding of the logical character of propositions about the present, the past and the future, they may also serve, and are sometimes intended to serve, a different purpose. To say that time is unreal is to ask us not to exaggerate the importance of what lies immediately before our eyes, to have a wider perspective in which what is remote is given its due importance and in which what lies before us here and now is better understood by being related to its antecedents and its consequences. Once again we find a philosophical remark serving as a reminder, this time as a reminder of how much the understanding of any one thing or event is a matter of seeing it in relation to other things and other events. The extreme extrapolation of this reminder is the idea that everything is connected with everything else, that we cannot fully understand anything unless we have understood everything. No piece of the jig-saw puzzle is correctly placed in its relation to all the other pieces until every piece is correctly placed in its relation to all the other pieces.

These reminders are hidden in paradoxes, but they can be detached from the paradoxical forms in which they are expressed. Wisdom has given plainer expression to part of what some of the traditional metaphysicians meant by the unreality of time when he has reminded us that in reading *Anna Karenina* for the sixth or seventh time we understand the beginning of the novel better because we now know what end it will reach, and by what steps it will reach that end.

The distinction between a form of words and the use or uses to which it can be put is as important here as it was in considering the contrast between ancient and modern uses of theological forms of words, and here too we must beware of thinking that a doctrine has been refuted in all its forms when it has been shown to be false if understood in its most literal sense. Before we dismiss an ancient metaphysical system we must consider what concrete application can be given to the abstract terms in which it is expressed. When we do this we shall usually find that it has an epistemological content that can be re-expressed in directly epistemological terms. We shall often find that it is also well adapted to serve the purpose of reminding us of something that is relevant to our lives and thoughts outside the scope of pure epistemology.

When we speak platitudinously of the need to broaden our minds we are travelling part of the route that Spinoza was following in the *Ethics*. He says much more, and he says it very differently, but that was part of the purpose for which he was assembling reminders. The more nearly a man approaches a complete understanding of the world the more nearly, according to Spinoza, will his conduct approach the ideal impartiality that is both virtue and knowledge, both happiness and wisdom.

A poem by W. H. Auden provides a typical example of the effort of memory and realization, of recalling what is known but half-forgotten, that is characteristic of the most elementary and the most fundamental understanding in philosophy, science, morality and religion:

> Night falls on China; the great arc of travelling shadow
> Moves over land and ocean, altering life:
> Thibet already silent, the packed Indias cooling.
>
> *Some Poems*, 1940, p. 79

Auden here spells out for himself his familiar matter-of-fact knowledge of the rotation of the earth, reminds himself that the sun is always rising and always setting, and at the same time he thinks of all sorts and conditions of men, remembers their manifold griefs and hopes, joys and fears. He widens his perspective without coming to know anything that he did not know already.

This example connects directly with one of Spinoza's illustrations of his theory of error (*Ethics*, II, 35, Scholium). If I look at the sun without knowing its distance from the earth, I may imagine it to be a small disc about 200 feet away. When I know that it is 90 million miles from the earth, it still *looks* to me as it looked before. And to know its size and distance is to know among other things that it will look to a being like myself placed on the earth as if it were a small disc 200 feet away. My initial idea is incomplete, but in its positive content it is correct: 'In ideas there is nothing positive on account of which they are called false' (*Ethics*, II, 33).

Unless we are blinded by the admittedly striking differences of idiom, we can recognize a close kinship between the aims and achievements of rationalist and idealistic metaphysicians like Spinoza and Bradley and the aims and achievements of their recent successors, even those of such an openly anti-rationalist and anti-idealistic temper as the positivists of the Vienna Circle. One of the main planks in the positivist platform has always been the ideal of a unified science. An attachment to this same ideal underlies much of the philosophy of Spinoza and the philosophy of Leibniz. The facile criticisms to which coherence theories of truth have recently been subjected underestimate the value of those theories as expressions of a determination to achieve a comprehensive understanding of the world, to look for connections and unity where at first sight there appear to be only multiplicity and diversity. The desire that comprehension should be comprehensive, though it is dressed in many different costumes in different times and different places, is common to the rationalist metaphysician, the positivist epistemologist, the theoretical scientist and the religious, moral, philosophical or literary thinker who wishes to achieve a perspective on life and man and the world.

Here I can give only one or two examples of the translation into the concrete of this pervasive desire for unity and connectedness. In a discussion some years ago Mr Gerd Buchdahl propounded the question, 'Is it conceivable that roses should grow on the moon?' The conventional empiricist will say at once that of course it is conceivable that roses should grow on the moon. It is a mere matter of contingent empirical fact that they do not grow there. We can easily imagine what it would be like to find them growing there. This is no doubt correct, but if we examine the question more closely we find that it is also seriously inadequate. It hides much of what we can learn by considering the question further and more seriously. If we were to place what looked like a rose tree into the barren rock on the moon's surface, and it grew and flourished there, we should have strong reason to doubt its claim to be an ordinary rose tree. Anything that was *unquestionably* a rose tree would wither and die in the absence of atmosphere, moisture and soil. On the other hand, if we equip the moon with atmosphere, moisture and soil, so that ordinary roses would grow there, we shall be changing it so radically that in the end it will become doubtful whether it is still the moon on which the roses are now growing and blooming.

Mr Buchdahl's example was no doubt meant to illustrate, as it does amply illustrate, the interdependence between our actual knowledge and the concepts in and through which we express it. Rationalist and idealist metaphysicians have vividly reminded us of that same interdependence, and we are gravely misreading them if we allow their modes of expression to obscure from us the character of what they wished to convey. When they paradoxically suggest that every true factual statement is such that its falsehood is inconceivable, or that only a complete account of the world could be completely true, their words are capable of expressing a falsehood. But we can recognize the falsehood of what these words may express without failing to recognize that the words are also capable of expressing something that is both true and important.

In our own everyday and philosophical usage we use the word 'inconceivable' not only to refer to what is self-contradictory, but also to refer to eventualities against whose actual occurrence the empirical evidence is overwhelming. It is inconceivable that in a place where there are seven times seven elephants there should not be forty-nine elephants. It is equally, though in a different sense, inconceivable that roses should grow on the moon. What is pointed out explicitly by Mr Buchdahl or another contemporary epistemologist is conveyed implicitly, but not necessarily therefore less clearly or effectively, by earlier metaphysicians in their own different idioms.

I have been told in outline of a piece of actual scientific research which teaches this same lesson. It is said that a team of botanists, who were studying the application of automatic computers to botanical taxonomy, fed into their computer a mass of data about the flora of a small region near Southampton, and then on the basis of the computer's analysis of the data

constructed a floral map of the region. They found to their grea
surprise that the distribution of species was such as to produc
on the floral map a clear and definite boundary which corres
ponded extremely closely with the boundary between tw
parishes. It was clear at once that this could not be a mer
coincidence, even though at first nobody was able to think c
any hypothesis that would connect a purely political boundar
with a difference in distribution of botanical species. Historica
research later revealed that at some time in the eighteent
century a new method of cultivation and drainage had bee.
introduced into one of the parishes, which had not been intro
duced into the other parish until twenty or thirty years late
The botanists were proceeding both scientifically and in accord
ance with common sense, but they were also proceeding i
accordance with the rationalist and idealist assumption that every
thing is connected with everything else: that there is indefinit
scope for finding new relations and connections between thing
that may appear at first sight to be entirely unrelated.

Philosophers who are so prompt and so perfunctory with thei
refutations of the coherence theory of truth might usefully reflec
on the notorious difficulty of sustained, continuous and con
sistent lying. No doubt it is theoretically possible to produce a
account of the world which is both false and internally coheren
but there is theoretical significance in the enormous practica
difficulty and indeed impossibility of doing so. Every strenuou
and sustained liar can be relied upon to contradict himself i
due course – a fact which is invaluable to detectives and court
of law. An infallible recipe for avoiding inconsistency is to stic
to saying what one knows for certain to be true.

Spinoza makes use of these insights not only in his though
about our understanding and knowledge of the world, bu
also in connection with our strivings for moral understandin
and self-knowledge. He identifies the complete freedom to
wards which he wishes man to aspire not only with complet
happiness but also with complete awareness and understandin
of the world. For Spinoza, as for Socrates, right action and righ
attitude are at one with complete knowledge and self-know
ledge. For Spinoza, partiality, in the sense in which its opposit
is impartiality, is identical with partiality in the sense in whic
it means *incompleteness*.

It was fashionable in the heyday of positivism to dismiss traditional metaphysics as 'mere literature'. This phrase itself suggests some obscure awareness of the parallel between metaphysics and literature to which I have drawn attention, but its dismissiveness also argues a blindness to the rational, cognitive character both of literature and of metaphysics. The kind of understanding of the world and man that is expressed in many works of traditional metaphysics is closely akin to the kind of understanding of ourselves and our situation to which *War and Peace* or *Paradise Lost* is designed to contribute. We have seen already that philosophy and theology overlap both in their scope and in their modes of operation. We can now see that in both respects each of them also overlaps with imaginative literature. This conclusion can be confirmed by looking at the philosophical themes and techniques of some writings that are undoubtedly works of literature rather than of philosophy, and also at the literary techniques and effects of some authors who are unmistakably and above all philosophers.

In Proust's work there are many passages of explicit philosophizing, about time, about memory, about our knowledge of other minds. In the strident music of Lawrence Durrell's *Alexandria Quartet* a recurrent theme is the radically new light in which one person may gradually or suddenly come to see another, and Durrell repeatedly wonders, through his narrators, whether any of us can ever really know anything at all about any other person. Tolstoy's preoccupation with freedom and determinism outcrops at the end of *War and Peace* in a formal essay on the philosophy of history, but this theme is less systematically and more effectively treated in the structure and texture of the novel itself. Again and again we find that what metaphysical philosophy does abstractly and generally is done by literature with concrete particularity. I have already referred in this connection to Professor E. A. Havelock's *Preface to Plato*. When Plato set himself to put all knowledge on a firm philosophical basis, and to express its essence through a theory of abstract universal Forms, he necessarily became involved in conflict with the sources and media which had been for the Greeks the sources and media of their understanding of the world. It was by learning their literature that Plato's predecessors and contemporaries were initiated into the knowledge

and understanding that was the religious and moral heritag
of their people. Even in our post-Platonic age we continue t
learn about ourselves and others from works of literature, an
the literature that we continue to learn from includes th
literature of the Greeks.

We still learn from the works of Plato himself, which ar
classics both of philosophy and of literature. Plato's dialogue
are another major example of the kind of pure and applie
philosophy that I have briefly illustrated by my references t
Spinoza and to Bradley. It is notorious that Plato's explici
opposition to literature was the expression of a conflict withi
himself. His war against the poets and the orators and th
tragedians was a civil war. The understanding of life and th
world that he offers to us is offered in and through a series o
works of imaginative literature. He portrays the life and deatl
of Socrates as paradigms of life and death. His media and hi
techniques are different from those of Homer or Sophocles, bu
his motives and purposes are not wholly different from their:
In his work we see a locus of intersection between literatur
philosophy and religion. The ideal world of the Forms, th
native land of the true philosopher, occupies in his system th
place that was occupied in Homer by Olympus and the gods o
the traditional pantheon. It is through the life and death o
Socrates, as well as through explicit, discursive philosophizin
that Plato commends to us and tries to set clearly before us th
coincidence that he saw or imagined between justice and i
reward; the Socratic message that complete knowledge is th
same as complete virtue and complete happiness, that, i
Spinoza's words, *Beatitudo non est virtutis praemium, sed ips*
virtus (*Ethics*, V, 42).

In the *Gorgias* and the *Phaedo* and the *Phaedrus* Plato presen
a literary portrait of the soul's nature and history and fate
His metaphysical two-world picture of the Forms above and th
shadowy phenomenal world below is a literary, analogic:
presentation of a view of life. To say that the Forms alone ar
real, and that the material world below is a passing shadow,
one way of saying that the things of the mind are more im
portant and more to be sought and prized than the things of th
flesh. The doctrine of *anamnesis* can be construed as a pictori:
expression of what we have seen to be a literal fact: that mor:

and religious and philosophical understanding is achieved by remembering and reviewing what we had known but half forgotten rather than by coming to know what we had in no sense known before. Plato says that every human soul has seen the Forms, and he hopes by his teaching to restore to men the clear vision that the body's life on earth has clouded. The philosopher's journey is not the exploration of a new and alien country. It is a homecoming to the land of his earliest memories, of which he was deprived by a birth that is but a sleep and a forgetting. Like the Christian theologian, Plato tells us that the victory is assured if only we strive for it, for he too believes that the victory for which he strives was won before his strife began.

Neither Plato nor the orthodox Christian will allow that his moral message can be abstracted from its doctrinal setting. Platonism is itself a religion, and while it may lack a *theology* it is certainly not 'in search of a metaphysic.' But it is a religion that may continue to be used by one who has abandoned its metaphysical ontology. There are and always have been many whose view of life and understanding of the world is Platonist, but who would not be prepared to accept, and might even be prepared to reject, and to claim that they could refute, the ontological, metaphysical doctrines which Plato himself regarded as an indispensable basis for his view of life.

I suggest that Arnold and Braithwaite and the Bishop of Woolwich make use of Christian terms and categories in the same sense that these latter-day Platonists make use of the philosophy and religion of Plato. Just as the modern Platonist may adhere to Plato's religion while abandoning Plato's metaphysics, so they adhere to the Christian religion while abandoning its theology. The Bishop of Woolwich has taken up Bonhoeffer's cry of 'Christianity without religion', but what he offers is more accurately to be described as the Christian religion without theology.

Kierkegaard is only one of many who have traced out more fully the parallels on which I am here relying. For some the life and death of Socrates have occupied the role that is fulfilled for others by the life and death of Christ. The *Phaedo* is Plato's gospel, and the drinking of the hemlock a voluntary and inescapable crucifixion.

Philosophy in the style of Plato or Spinoza is no longer

done with conviction, because the ontological doctrines on which they based their conclusions about life and conduct can no longer be constructed with conviction. But Plato and Spinoza are still read with attention, not only for their contribution to pure philosophy but also for the help they give us in enquiries that transcend the limits of technical philosophy. Just as we continue to use the mythology and theology of ancient Greece as media for developing and expressing our understanding of life and the world, though we have long ceased to believe in the literal truth of the underlying doctrines, so we can continue to use the philosophy of Spinoza or Plato to express and extend our understanding of ourselves and our situation even when we have ceased either to believe in their metaphysical doctrines or to attempt to replace them by rival doctrines of the same nature.

Christianity is in the same case. It embodies insights which were thought by its authors to depend on the truth of certain transcendentalist doctrines. Arnold is a proof, and Braithwaite and the Bishop of Woolwich are a living proof, that Christianity can survive as a medium for the conduct of reflection about men and their lives and their perplexities, even when a belief in its transcendentalist propositions has been abandoned. And to recognize that this is a function that Christian theology shares with philosophy and literature is not to demean Christianity but to restore to philosophy and literature the importance that has sometimes in recent decades been denied to them even by their exponents and apologists.

The poet, the dramatist and the novelist, the philosopher, the moralist and the theologian, are still needed and will for many centuries, if not for ever, continue to be needed, to supplement the inquiries and discoveries of more formal and specialized investigators. Even in the sphere of strictly factual enquiry there are questions that cannot be remitted to professional natural scientists. Human nature is an important part of nature, and a part of nature that no natural science has unchallengeably annexed. The more informal but not necessarily less disciplined reflections of philosophers and theologians and men of letters are still possible and necessary supplements to the investigations of psychologists and sociologists. When we add to this the other function that is to be attributed to the literary and moral sciences, the function of trying to achieve some perspective on human knowledge as a whole, to see the various aspects of human experience in relation to each other and to the results of the more special arts and sciences, we can see how grave a mistake is made by those who look only to specialized experts for insight, knowledge and understanding.

It is just because informal reflection of this kind is not the preserve of any specialized profession that it is liable to be despised and neglected by those who have their own special and professional fields to cultivate. Professionals in any field are jealous of the attempts of non-professionals to pursue understanding and knowledge, and their jealousies are re-inforced, and given some show of justification, by the fact that most of the amateurs are so grossly amateurish. But the cure for the bad conduct of this or any other kind of inquiry is not to abandon it, but to do it better, and we shall never do it better if we believe that it cannot be done at all. A search for know-ledge and understanding cannot be pursued effectively except by those who recognize that it *is* a search for knowledge and understanding, and that it seeks for what is capable of being found; that even in the remainder class of problems outside all specialisms there is scope for seeking and the hope of finding truth and knowledge, and that the search for this as for all other knowledge and truth, however specialized, is objective, is amenable and responsive to the use of the human reason and understanding.

We have already considered the two modes of thought and apprehension that are especially characteristic of the best work in this field – the work of the greatest philosophers, poets and prophets. They are two modes of exploration of the familiar. One consists in the perception of hitherto unrecognized patterns in the otherwise bewildering and variegated details of facts that are themselves well known but imperfectly understood in their relations one to another. The other is the striving, no less rational for being also imaginative, to achieve a vivid realiza-tion of the truth of what are already recognized as truths. Both these modes of thought, when misconducted or imperfectly understood, contribute to the propagation of the half-truth that philosophers do nothing but repeat themselves and each other from generation to generation. This half-truth and its twin are both well understood by T. E. Hulme:

It is as impossible to discover anything new about the ways of man in regard to the cosmos as it is to observe anything new about the ways of a kitten. The general conceptions we can form are as limited in number as the possible gestures of the dance, and as fixed in type as is the physiology of man himself. The philosopher who has not been anticipated in this sense of the word does not exist, or, if he does, he breathes forth his wisdom in the ineffectual silence of solitary confinement.

But if that is so, what is the use of bothering about the matter at all? Why should you investigate even the relatively new? Just as one generation after another is content to watch the eternally fixed and constant antics of kittens, so one might urge, should one generation after another be content to watch the antics of the philosophers without sighing after anything new. There is this obvious objection: that while the antics of the kitten, like the art of the actor, die with it, the same is not true of philosophers.

It is necessary for the kittens of this generation to repeat the gestures of the past in order that we may see them at all, for the dead kittens who did the same things are gone beyond recall; but in philosophy the gestures of the dead are recorded in print. What justification is there for philosophy if it does nought but repeat the same old attitudes? This is a plausible but fallacious objection, and based on an illusion. The phrases of dead philosophers recorded in print are to most people as dead as dead kittens. In order that they may appear alive they must be said over again in the phraseology of the moment. This, then, is the only originality left to a philosopher – the invention of a new dialect in which to restate an old attitude.

Further Speculations, p. 3[

Philosophy consists in the assembling of reminders, and one cannot remind somebody of something unless he already know it. The pursuit of wisdom, the search for vision, largely consists, as Plato well knew, in the attempt to achieve re-vision recollection, *anamnesis*. And a large part of what we have to remember both in this and in other philosophical inquiries is that the railways of conventional thought, while they facilitat movement, do so at the cost of limiting its range and direction. Wisdom's child at the theatre misses what he misses because his mind is not moulded to fit the networks of conventional understanding; but it is for the same reason that he sees what he sees.

When Socrates pronounced that the unexamined life was not worth living he was calling his hearers to engage in reflection of the informal kind that I have been describing, to take stock, to recall and review what was in their minds or before their eyes. Arnold makes the same plea in *Culture and Anarchy* when he asks for the application to moral questions of the thought and effort that we all know we must give to our non-moral perplexities. Socrates and Arnold are here themselves assembling reminders, and we need their reminders because we are so easily tempted to play down the role of reason and intelligence in these spheres. We are an easy prey to the specialist superstition that nothing is a use of the reason unless it is a formal and technical use, guided and governed by the principles and methods of some specialized department of inquiry, some organized and official search for knowledge.

That this is a mistake can be seen by looking at the progress in knowledge and understanding that a child makes in his earliest years, and at how much of it is progress in 'finding his way about' rather than in the acquisition of facts and information. The child at the theatre is learning new facts, but he is also extending his grasp of facts already known to him, coming to understand much that he had learned and could repeat but had not inwardly digested. To ask us to become as little children, to be born again, is among other things to urge us to strive for liberation from the nets of conventional thought, for the restoration of a pristine freshness of apprehension; though we must at the same time beware of losing what we have caught in those nets. It is no more negligible than what slips through their meshes.

It has often been noticed that a philosopher's questions are like those of a child. It has not so often been recognized that children's questions divide themselves into the same two kinds as the philosopher's questions. Children characteristically suffer from *epistemological* perplexities. They are puzzled and sometimes troubled by the questions that become for the professional philosopher the technical material of his trade.

'How can I ever know what you are thinking?' 'Is our house still there when I am at school?' But children also feel and sometimes express those perplexities about the problems of life that are the province of the informal, unofficial philosopher of life.

A philosopher of either kind is one who goes on asking the questions that most people stop asking when they grow up. If he is prepared to remain childish, childlike, as Socrates was childlike, there need be no limit to the progress he can continue to make in acquiring a mode of understanding that is inaccessible to those who have put away childish things.

This connection is marked by Francis Thompson in his essay on Shelley:

> Coming to Shelley's poetry, we peep over the wild mask of revolutionary metaphysics, and we see the winsome face of the child. Perhaps none of his poems is more purely and typically Shelleian than *The Cloud*, and it is interesting to note how essentially it springs from the faculty of make-believe. The same thing is conspicuous, though less purely conspicuous, throughout his singing; it is the child's faculty of make-believe raised to the nth power. He is still at play, save only that his play is such as manhood stops to watch, and his playthings are those which the gods give their children. The universe is his box of toys. *Works*, *III*, 17–18.

Thompson does not further or fully express the richness of his own analogy. For Spinoza the world is one vast jigsaw puzzle, which is 'guaranteed fully interlocking'. It is a puzzle with a unique and complete solution: when we have fitted all the pieces together we shall see the unique, unitary, unified picture of God-or-Nature. For the empiricist philosopher, the world is more like a set of Hornby trains or Meccano pieces. Man is represented by this school of philosophy as building up his world, constructing or logically constructing it out of ideas or sense-data or atomic facts or *Protokollsätze*. Here there is no aspiration after a unique and definitive solution, as of a jigsaw puzzle, but rather of the indefinite additions and extensions that can be made to a Hornby train system or to a collection of Meccano.

The conflict between jigsaw puzzle philosophers and

Meccano philosophers is not confined to disputes about our knowledge of the external world. It recurs in the opposition between conventionalists and Platonists about the nature of mathematics and logic – the conflict between the picture of mathematicians as inventors or constructors and the picture of them as explorers or discoverers. We have considered earlier the analogous dispute between the subjectivist and objectivist representations of the character of moral inquiry. In all these and all other metaphysical fields there is perennial debate between the creativists, the constructivists, and the defenders of the claims of all these inquiries to be branches of positive and objective knowledge, whose results are not fashioned but found.

We have come full circle, and in our end as in our beginning we encounter the problem of the One and the Many; the ancient but not insoluble problem of reconciling the manifold variety of the modes of understanding and knowledge with their unity and community as modes of *understanding* and of *knowledge*. This has been the theme of this whole book: that between this unity and this variety there is no conflict. A conception of the unity of knowledge that requires us severely to limit the variety of knowledge must be a misconception of its unity. And the same misconception of its unity is the only plausible basis there could be for supposing that its evident variety fragments and disunites it.

To insist that God cannot be beyond reason and above truth is not to ask that God be narrowed and lowered but to ask that reason and truth be seen in their full breadth and height and depth.

Like Wisdom's child we must try to remember what we usually forget without forgetting what we usually remember: like him 'we need to be at once like someone who has seen much and forgotten nothing, and also like one who is seeing everything for the first time'.

Bibliography

A list of books and articles quoted or referred to in the text.

ARNOLD, MATTHEW, *Literature and Dogma*, London 1873
— *Culture and Anarchy*, London 1869
AYER, A. J. *Language, Truth and Logic*, London 1947
BAMBROUGH, RENFORD, 'Universals and Family Resemblances', *Proceedings of the Aristotelian Society*, 1960–61
— 'Principia Metaphysica', *Philosophy*, 1964
— 'Unanswerable Questions', *Proceedings of the Aristotelian Society, Supplementary Volume*, 1966
— 'Aristotle on Justice: a Paradigm of Philosophy', in Bambrough (ed.) *New Essays on Plato and Aristotle*, London 1965
BONHOEFFER, DIETRICH, *Letters and Papers from Prison*, London 1953
BRADLEY, F. H., *Ethical Studies*, Oxford 1927
— *Principles of Logic*, Oxford 1922
— *Appearance and Reality*, Oxford 1897
BRAITHWAITE, R. B., *An Empiricist's View of the Nature of Religious Belief*, Cambridge 1955
BROAD, C. D., *The Mind and Its Place in Nature*, London 1925
EMMET, DOROTHY, *Presuppositions and Finite Truths*, London 1949
FLEW, A. G. N. and MACINTYRE, A. C., *New Essays in Philosophical Theology*, London 1955
FREUD, SIGMUND, *New Introductory Lectures on Psycho-analysis*, London 1933
HANSON, N. R., *Patterns of Discovery*, Cambridge 1958
HARE, R. M., *The Language of Morals*, Oxford 1952
— *Freedom and Reason*, Oxford 1963
HAVELOCK, E. A., *Preface to Plato*, Oxford 1963
HULME, T. E., *Speculations*, London 1924
— *Further Speculations*, Minneapolis 1955
HUME, DAVID, *Enquiries*, edited by L. A. Selby-Bigge, Oxford 1902
— *Dialogues Concerning Natural Religion*, edited by Norman Kemp Smith, London 1947
JAMES, WILLIAM, *The Varieties of Religious Experience*, London 1902
KANT, IMMANUEL, *Religion Within the Limits of Reason Alone*, New York 1960

LEWIS, C. S., *A Preface to Paradise Lost*, Oxford 1942
MACKINNON, D. M., *A Study in Ethical Theory*, London 1957
MALCOLM, NORMAN, *Ludwig Wittgenstein: A Memoir*, London 1958
MILL, J. S., *A System of Logic*, London 1843
MONTEFIORE, ALAN, 'Goodness and Choice', *Proceedings of the Aristotelian Society, Supplementary Volume*, 1961
MOORE, G. E., *Philosophical Papers*, London 1959
NEWELL, R. W., *The Concept of Philosophy*, London 1967
NOWELL-SMITH, P. H., *Ethics*, Harmondsworth 1954
POUND, EZRA, *Literary Essays*, London 1954
PRICHARD, H. A., *Moral Obligation*, Oxford 1949
RAMSEY, F. P., *The Foundations of Mathematics*, London 1931
ROBINSON, JOHN A. T., *Honest to God*, London 1963
RUSSELL, BERTRAND, *The Problems of Philosophy*, London 1912
— *Human Knowledge, Its Scope and Limits*, London 1948
SARTRE, J.-P., *Existentialism and Humanism*, London 1948
SPINOZA, B., *Ethics*, The Hague 1882
STEVENSON, CHARLES L., 'Ethical Judgments and Avoidability', *Mind*, 1938
— *Facts and Values*, New Haven 1963
THOMPSON, FRANCIS, *Collected Works*, Volume III, London 1913
TILLICH, PAUL, *The Shaking of the Foundations*, London 1949
WILLIAMS, W. T. and LAMBERT, J. M., 'Multivariate methods in plant ecology. I. Association-analysis in plant communities', *The Journal of Ecology*, Vol. 47, No. 1, March, 1959
WINTERS, YVOR, *In Defense of Reason*, London 1960
WISDOM, JOHN *Philosophy and Psycho-analysis*, Oxford 1953
— *Other Minds*, Oxford 1965
— *Paradox and Discovery*, Oxford 1965
WITTGENSTEIN, LUDWIG, *Philosophical Investigations*, Oxford 1953
— *The Blue and Brown Books*, Oxford 1958

Bibliographical Note

I have been unable to trace a published reference to the botanical example used on pp. 147–8. There is little doubt that it derives from the work of Professor W. T. Williams and his colleagues, and I have therefore listed one of their papers on some parallel cases. I am grateful to Dr G. C. Evans, Dr S. M. Walters and Dr D. E. Coombe for their help and advice in this connection.

Index